SURVEY OF THE SCRIPTURES
BASIC BIBLE COMMENTARY

The New Testament

Matthew through Revelation

Dr. Alfred Martin

MERIDIAN
PUBLICATIONS

Copyright © 1989 by Meridian

New edition printed in 1995 by Meridian

Published by special arrangement with and permission of Moody External Studies. Revised edition by Moody External Studies of the USA.

First edition by Moody Bible Institute of the USA. All rights reserved.

No part of this book may be reproduced in any form without written permission from Moody Bible Institute, 820 N. La Salle Dr., Chicago, IL 60610.

First edition © 1961 by Moody Bible Institute

This edition has been adapted for those not enrolled in Moody External Studies. The New King James Version of the Bible (NKJV), copyright © Thomas Nelson, Inc., 1990, has been used for verses with archaic English words; otherwise the King James Version (KJV) is used.

M0007 Paperback Study Edition
ISBN 156570-000-7

Cover design by Gayle Raymer
Book Design by Blue Water Ink

A Meridian Publication
Manufactured in the United States of America

Contents

Preface

Just as a heart specialist must understand the rudiments of biology and human physiology before exploring the intricacies of the cardiovascular system, so we must understand how the entire Bible fits together before we can comprehend the specifics of it.

Survey of the Scriptures is a tour through the Bible that points out how one section relates to another, each subject to the whole. By knowing how each part relates to the others, we can better appreciate and apply the lessons of the whole Bible.

Meridian titles in addition to *The New Testament—Matthew through Revelation* in the *Survey of the Scriptures* currently include:

Matthew—Gospel of the King
John—Life through Believing
Acts—Power for Witnessing
Romans—Amazing Grace
Revelation—God's Final Word to Man

Additional titles in the *Survey of the Scriptures* series are forthcoming.

For many years Dr. Alfred Martin taught these *Survey of the Scriptures* as "Bible 101" at Moody Bible Institute, then later at Dallas Bible Institute and Southern Bible Institute. For over thirty years the summary of his work has been published as a Bible correspondence course for the External Studies Division of Moody Bible Institute.

Now for the first time this incisive and insightful study is available for personal or group Bible study. It will help students see the Scriptures as an interrelated unit with a plan and a purpose.

Thirty years ago I graduated from Moody Bible Institute with a foundation in God's Word built on *Survey of the Scriptures*. As Dr. Martin then opened to me a new understanding and appreciation of the Bible, I now am proud to be able to publish his survey materials so that you too can better appreciate how each portion of God's Word fits into the whole.

—The Publisher.

*I*ntroduction

To see the Bible as a whole is not only vital to a proper understanding of the Bible; it is also a thrilling experience!

Survey of the Scriptures, first written as a Bible study course and used as a basic text in Bible 101, is based in part on a course by Dr. James M. Gray, past president of Moody Bible Institute. Dr. Martin quotes Dr. Gray throughout the *Survey.* Maps and charts were prepared by John Phillips, author of several "Exploring the Scriptures" titles. John Phillips was director of both Moody and Emmaus correspondence schools.

The content of this edition is taken from an adult credit course from Moody Bible Institute, External Studies Division. For information on how you might take this and other courses for credit, write for a free catalog to:

Moody External Studies
Moody Bible Institute
820 N. La Salle
Chicago, IL 60610

The New Testament

The Old Testament was written in preparation for the coming of the Lord Jesus Christ into the world. The last book of the Old Testament, Malachi, shows the promise still unfulfilled.

For about four hundred years after Malachi, the people of Israel received no direct message from God. During this time they were largely under foreign domination, as had been prophesied in the book of Daniel. The godly remnant in Israel confidently looked for the coming of the promised Redeemer.

The New Testament, which records the coming of the Lord Jesus Christ into the world, is made up of twenty-seven books. Generally we think of these as being in three main divisions: five books of history—the four gospels, and the book of Acts; twenty-one letters, or epistles, from Romans through Jude; and one book of prophecy, Revelation. These twenty-seven books, written by eight or nine writers, complete God's revelation. The opening verses of the letter to the Hebrews (1:1–2 NKJV) portray the comparison and the contrast between the Old Testament and the New: "God, who at various times and in various ways spoke in time past to the fathers by the prophets [this refers to the Old Testament], has in these last days spoken unto us by His Son" [this is recorded in the New Testament].

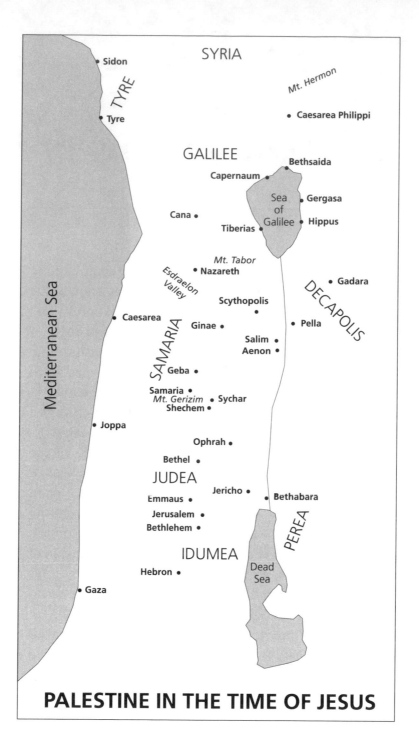

PALESTINE IN THE TIME OF JESUS

1

History

The first four books of the New Testament are commonly called the four gospels. These are four records given by God of the earthly life and ministry, crucifixion, and resurrection of his Son, the Lord Jesus Christ. The accounts supplement one another. The first three—Matthew, Mark, and Luke—are often called the Synoptic Gospels, from a Greek expression meaning "to see together." Hence, they are parallel in many respects.

No one of the gospel records professes to tell everything about the Lord Jesus. Each has its particular emphasis and is designed by God for a particular group of readers. Matthew, originally addressed primarily to the Jews, presents Jesus Christ as the King. Mark, written primarily for the Romans, presents him as the Servant. Luke, appealing primarily to the Greeks, presents him as the perfect Man. The Gospel of John, written many years after the other three and emphasizing different aspects of Christ's ministry, is addressed to all men and presents the Lord Jesus as God.

It would be a mistake, however, to think that any one of the gospels is addressed exclusively to one group of people or that it contains only one of these four aspects of Christ's person and work. All of the gospels are, in the last analysis, for all men; and they all present the Lord Jesus Christ as King, as Servant, as perfect Man, and as God. It is simply the emphasis in each that is different.

THE GOSPEL OF MATTHEW

The writer of the first gospel was one of the twelve apostles, Matthew, who was also called Levi (Matthew 9:9; Mark 2:14; Luke 5:27–29). He was a tax gatherer for the Roman government when the Lord Jesus called him into his service.

The gospel of Matthew presents the Lord Jesus Christ as the fulfiller of two great covenants of the Old Testament: the Abrahamic Covenant, in which God promised that in a descendant of Abraham all the families of the earth should be blessed; and the Davidic Covenant, in which God promised that David would never lack a man to sit upon his throne (Genesis 12:1–3; 2 Samuel 7:5–17). Christ is seen in the book primarily as the King, the descendant of David.

Matthew may be outlined as follows:

1. GENEALOGY, BIRTH, AND CHILDHOOD OF THE KING (chapters 1– 2)

2. THE KINGDOM AT HAND (chapters 3–12)

3. THE PARABLES OF THE KING (chapter 13)

4. WITHDRAWAL OF THE KING IN VIEW OF HIS COMING REJECTION (chapters 14–18)

5. APPROACH OF THE KING TOWARD HIS OFFICIAL REJECTION (chapters 19–23)

6. THE PROPHECIES OF THE KING
    (chapters 24–25)

7. ARREST, TRIAL, DEATH, BURIAL, AND
    RESURRECTION OF THE KING (chapters 26–28)

1. Genealogy, Birth, and Childhood of the King (chapters 1–2)

The opening of Matthew's gospel shows the official title of the Lord Jesus to the throne of David by tracing his legal descent from David and his right as the fulfiller of the Abrahamic Covenant because of his descent from Abraham. The virgin birth of Christ is fully declared and indicated to be a fulfillment of the prophecy of Isaiah 7:14 (Matthew 1:23).

The accounts of the nativity in Matthew and Luke supplement each other. The visit of the wise men, so often misinterpreted, must have taken place some months at least after the birth of the Lord Jesus. This seems clear because, while they were far away in the East, the wise men saw the star that announced the Savior's birth. Furthermore, the mention of the house and the young child is quite different from Luke's account of the newborn Babe in the manger. This section closes with the flight into Egypt and the return to Nazareth after the death of Herod.

2. The Kingdom at Hand (chapters 3–12)

The gospel of Matthew, as has been said, is appropriately known as *The Gospel of the King.* In it the Lord Jesus is proclaimed as Israel's King—first, by his herald, or forerunner, John the Baptizer; then by his own announcement as he began his public ministry; and later by the proclamation of his apostles. This book may also be called *The Gospel of Rejection,* for it denotes, almost from its outset, the almost universal and sometimes violent rejection of the Lord Jesus. The ministry of John the Baptizer (announcing that the kingdom is at hand) is followed by Christ's baptism and his temptation by Satan. As he began his public ministry, Christ proclaimed the same message that John had preached: "Repent: for the kingdom of heaven is at hand" (4:17). The expression, *the kingdom of heaven,* found only in the gospel of Matthew, seems to be based on a passage in the book of Daniel which prophesies that the God of heaven shall set up a kingdom (Daniel 2:44).

Matthew does not tell of the early ministry of the Lord in Judea, but goes at once to the great Galilean ministry and devotes a large amount of space to that. In chapters 5–7 in his great discourse, usually known as the Sermon on the Mount, Christ sets forth the laws of his Kingdom. The Sermon on the Mount is not intended to show the way of salvation but proclaims principles of living for those who belong to the Lord Jesus. Following his statement of the laws of his Kingdom, the King performs mighty miracles in fulfillment of Old Testament prophecies (chapters 8–9), sends forth his messengers (chapter 10) and announces his credentials (chapters 11–12). Official rejection of the King by the nation of Israel is foreshadowed when the Pharisees accuse him of doing his mighty works through the power of Satan (9:34). Their attack is intensified (12:24), and the coming rejection of the Lord is clearly evident.

3. The Parables of the King (chapter 13)

In a series of seven parables the Lord Jesus sets forth the "mysteries of the kingdom of heaven" (13:11). During the King's absence the Kingdom exists in mystery form as the sphere of profession, containing that which is false as well as that which is true. Evil will gradually permeate this sphere, as symbolized by the parable of the leaven, and eventually there will be a separation of the false from the true, as foretold in the parables of the wheat and the tares and the dragnet. Chapter 13 closes with the rejection of the Lord Jesus at Nazareth, the place where he had been brought up.

4. Withdrawal of the King in View of His Coming Rejection (chapters 14–18)

The death of John the Baptizer led Christ to retire from his ministry in the cities. The account of the miracle of the feeding of the five thousand (14:15–21)—the only miracle recorded in all four of the gospels—is later paralleled by the miracle of the feeding of the four thousand (15:32–39). The Lord Jesus warns against the leaven of the Pharisees and Sadducees, by which he means their teaching (16:12); and near Caesarea Philippi he calls forth the great confession from Peter, "You are the Christ, the Son of the living God" (Matthew 16:16). Here he announces for the first time his purpose to build his church and begins to predict his death and resurrection. The transfiguration scene (17:1–13) is a preview of the coming millennial Kingdom. The Lord continues to announce his impending death (17:22–23) and teaches humility and forgiveness (chapter 18).

5. Approach of the King toward His Official Rejection (chapters 19–23)

The events described in chapters 19–23 take place during the closing months of the Lord Jesus' ministry, as he looks toward his death on the cross. On the way to Jerusalem for the final visit, he again warns his disciples of what is to come (20:18–19). In chapter 21, he is in the final week of his earthly ministry before the crucifixion. In his entry into the city he consciously and deliberately fulfills the prophecy of Zechariah 9:9 (Matthew 21:4–5). Teaching during that week in the temple and elsewhere, the Lord Jesus answers questions of his critics and asks them a question concerning the person of the Messiah, which they are unable to answer (22:41–46). His sharp denunciation of the scribes and Pharisees as hypocrites (chapter 23) is followed by his sad lament over the city of Jerusalem (23:37–39).

6. The Prophecies of the King (chapters 24–25)

The words of the Lord Jesus in these chapters are ordinarily known as the Olivet Discourse because he spoke them from the Mount of Olives. In this message he traces the course of history, answering particularly the question of the disciples concerning the end time and his coming again. His return will result in judgment on the nation of Israel and on the Gentile nations.

7. Arrest, Trial, Death, Burial, and Resurrection of the King (chapters 26–28)

The rejection of Christ, which has been evident throughout the Gospel of Matthew, comes to a climax in this section as he is betrayed by Judas Iscariot, arrested, brought before the council, denied by Peter, delivered to the Roman governor, and finally tortured and crucified. After all this it seemed hopeless that the Son of David would be able to fulfill his prophesied destiny, but the Lord Jesus Christ is also the Son of Abraham in whom all the nations of the world will be blessed. Coming forth from the grave in resurrection, he lives to fulfill both the Davidic Covenant and the Abrahamic Covenant. The gospel of Matthew closes with the Great Commission (Matthew 28:18–20), in which the Lord Jesus Christ sends his disciples forth to all nations.

To read and master the contents of this gospel is necessary and beneficial, but not sufficient. There must be a personal appropriation of the truth, a personal acceptance of the Lord

Jesus Christ, a personal confession, along with Simon Peter, "You are the Christ, the Son of the living God."

THE GOSPEL OF MARK

Since the first three gospels are parallel in many respects, it is unnecessary to call attention to all the events in each one. There are, however, distinctive features in each one that ought to be noted in connection with the other Synoptic Gospels.

Although the writer of this gospel is not mentioned in the book, early and continuous tradition ascribes it to John Mark, who is mentioned a number of times in the New Testament (see, for example, Acts 12:12; 13:5; 15:37; Philemon 24; 1 Peter 5:13). He was a cousin of Barnabas (Colossians 4:10 ASV), a companion of Paul, and also a close companion of Peter. It was in his mother's house that the church met when Peter was in prison (Acts 12:12). Early church writers stated that Mark wrote his gospel under the supervision of Peter, since Mark himself was not an eyewitness of the events recorded.

Mark is generally supposed to have been written primarily for the Romans. It contains comparatively few Old Testament references and explains a number of Jewish words and customs. (Note, for example, 5:41; 7:1–4; 7:34; 14:12, 15:42). The particular emphasis in Mark concerning the person and work of Christ is upon the fact that he was the perfect and faithful Servant. The book stresses deeds. The discourses of the Lord Jesus are, for the most part, omitted. Mark is the shortest of the four gospels. It contains no genealogy of the Lord Jesus and no reference to his birth or infancy. It begins with his ministry. A characteristic word is the one translated most often in the King James Version *straightway,* which means "immediately."

Mark is the gospel of action. Events move in rapid sequence. It has been suggested by many that Mark 10:45 may be regarded as a key verse of the book: "For even the Son of man came not to be ministered unto, but to minister, and to give his life a ransom for many. "The word *minister* means "to serve" or "to be a servant," and the two main thoughts in the book are these:

1. THE SON OF MAN MINISTERING (chapters 1–9)

2. THE SON OF MAN GIVING HIS LIFE AS A
   RANSOM (chapters 10–16)

There is a close connection between this gospel and the book of Isaiah, the Old Testament prophecy that presents the Lord Jesus Christ as the suffering Servant of Jehovah.

1. The Son of Man Ministering (chapters 1–9)

Like the other Synoptic Gospels, Mark devotes much space to the ministry of our Lord in Galilee. After the introduction (1:1–13), which tells of John the Baptist's ministry, the baptism of the Lord Jesus, and his temptation by Satan, the account opens with the preaching of the Lord Jesus in Galilee and the call of Simon and Andrew. Apparently the events follow in chronological order, with many mighty works and some parables. After Peter's confession at Caesarea Philippi, the Lord Jesus began to predict his death and resurrection (8:31). He repeated this after his transfiguration (9:31).

2. The Son of Man Giving His Life as a Ransom (chapters 10–16)

By the time the record reaches chapter 10, the Lord Jesus is on his final journey to Jerusalem, looking toward his approaching death. He makes specific reference again to this as the disciples journey toward the city (10:33–34).

The events beginning with chapter 11 pertain to the final week of our Lord's ministry. The account of the Crucifixion and the Resurrection, of course, is found in all four of the gospels. Mark parallels Matthew in giving the cry from the cross, "My God, my God, why have you forsaken me?" (15:34; compare Matthew 27:46). According to the final chapter, the Lord Jesus has risen from the dead and is to be proclaimed throughout the earth to every creature (16:15).

THE GOSPEL OF LUKE

We have seen that each of the four gospels has a specific purpose and presents the Lord Jesus Christ in a specific way. They are four aspects of the one perfect life. Luke emphasizes the perfect humanity of the Lord Jesus. The early church writers asserted that his gospel was written primarily for the Greeks, who were especially interested in the ideal Man. Luke is called in the Scriptures "the beloved physician" (Colossians 4:14). He was a companion of Paul at various times, from the occasion of Paul's departure from Troas on his second missionary journey. This is seen by the sections in the book of Acts that use the pronoun *we*, since Luke is the writer of that book as well.

Many students of the Scriptures have noted that Luke is a true historian. Evidence of this is seen in the introduction to his gospel. Both the gospel of Luke and the book of Acts are addressed to a friend, Theophilus, in order that Theophilus might know with all accuracy the life and ministry of the Lord Jesus and the beginning and spread of the church. As a historian, Luke gives dates for some of the pivotal events in the gospel. (Note 1:5, 2:1; 3:2, 23.)

The gospel of Luke has much unique material. A number of miracles are described only in Luke, and at least ten parables are peculiar to this gospel, including the familiar ones of the good Samaritan and the prodigal son.

W. H. Griffith Thomas has spoken of Luke as the gospel of praise. It begins and ends with joy. The first hymns of the Church are here: to use their Latin titles, *Magnificat* (1:46–55), *Benedictus* (1:68–79), *Gloria in Excelsis Deo* (2:14), and *Nunc Dimittis* (2:29–32).

Various writers have called attention to specific emphases in the gospel of Luke. It is the gospel of prayer. Two parables on persevering prayer are found only in Luke (11:5–13; 18:1–14). Christ's prayers at his baptism, after the cleansing of the leper, before the calling of the twelve apostles, at his transfiguration, on the cross for his murderers all are recorded in Luke. Some have called this the gospel of childhood because of the details given concerning the birth and childhood of the Lord Jesus Christ and John the Baptizer. It has been called the gospel of womanhood because of such records as those of Elisabeth (chapter 1); Mary, the mother of Jesus (chapters 1–2); the widow of Nain (7:12–15); the women who ministered to Christ (8:2–3); Mary and Martha (10:38–42); the weeping women on the way to the cross (23:27–31).

This is the Gospel to the whole world. Christ's ancestry is traced back to Adam (3:38). There are references to Gentiles and Samaritans, and there is an absence of Hebrew words such as are found in Matthew and Mark. It is believed that Luke himself was a Gentile. If so, he was the only Gentile writer of Scripture.

Christ is seen in Luke as the Son of Man. His words to Zacchaeus in 19:10 may be taken as a key verse of the book: "For the Son of man is come to seek and to save that which was lost." The gospel of Luke may be outlined as follows:

1. THE COMING AND PREPARATION OF
   THE SON OF MAN (1:1–4:13)

2. THE MINISTRY OF THE SON OF MAN
   IN GALILEE (4:14–9:50)

3. THE MINISTRY OF THE SON OF MAN IN PEREA,
   SAMARIA, AND JUDEA (9:51–19:27)

4. THE SUFFERING, DEATH, AND RESURRECTION
   OF THE SON OF MAN (19:28–24:53)

This is the only gospel that says anything about the boyhood of the Lord Jesus (2:40–52). The genealogy of Christ (3:23–38) is different from that in Matthew. While there are some difficulties of interpretation, it seems likely that Matthew, writing for Jews, connects the Lord Jesus Christ with Abraham and David, giving the *legal* line through Joseph, who was the legal father, although not the actual father, of Jesus. The genealogy in Luke is evidently the *natural* line of Mary, although her name is not given. It is likely that Heli was the father of Mary, the father-in-law of Joseph. The Lord Jesus Christ was the only person who could have inherited the throne of David because of the curse pronounced upon the line of Coniah, or Jehoiachin, in Jeremiah 22:30. (*Coniah* is a contraction of *Jeconiah*, 1 Chronicles 3:16.) Christ's legal right came through David's son, Solomon, down through the kings of Judah; but he avoided the curse upon the descendants of Coniah because his actual descent came through Mary, who was descended from David through Nathan. It was necessary that the Lord Jesus be born of a virgin and that this virgin be the wife of Joseph, who was of the legal line. If the Lord Jesus Christ had been the actual son of Joseph, there would have been a contradiction in the Scripture, and he would have been removed from the throne.

This gospel gives a much further account of the post-resurrection ministry of the Lord Jesus than do Matthew and

Mark. When the risen Lord appeared to the two disciples on the road to Emmaus, he showed them how he had fulfilled the Old Testament Scriptures: "And beginning at Moses and all the prophets, he expounded unto them in all the scriptures the things concerning himself" (24:27). Later, to the disciples he said: "All things must be fulfilled, which were written in the law of Moses, and in the prophets, and in the psalms, concerning me" (24:44). The book closes with the ascension , the event which begins the book of Acts.

THE GOSPEL OF JOHN

The gospel of John was written to tell people about the Lord Jesus Christ, the Son of God, in order that they might believe on him and thereby receive eternal life. Its purpose is stated in these words: "And many other signs truly did Jesus in the presence of his disciples, which are not written in this book: but these are written, that you might believe that Jesus is the Christ, the Son of God; and that believing you might have life through his name" (John 20:30–31).

The gospel of John was the last of the four to be written. Its writer is John, the son of Zebedee, who never refers to himself by name in the book, preferring to call himself the "disciple whom Jesus loved" (John 13:23; 19:26; 20:2; 21:7, 20, 24). John assumes that many of his readers already know the things written in the Synoptic Gospels. He omits almost entirely the ministry of the Lord Jesus in Galilee, although he does include some distinctive miracles there and stresses especially the Lord's ministry in Jerusalem and Judea.

Structure of the Book

In this book we read first of Christ's ministry to the world (chapters 1–12) and then of his ministry to his own followers (chapters 13–21).

24

We may outline the book this way:

1. PROLOGUE: THE ETERNAL WORD (1:1–19)

2. CHRIST'S MINISTRY TO THE WORLD (1:19–12:50)

3. CHRIST'S MINISTRY TO HIS OWN (13:1–17:26)

4. CHRIST'S DEATH AND RESURRECTION (18:1–20:31)

5. EPILOGUE: THE RISEN LORD (21:1–25)

Signs and Sayings

John stresses certain signs or miracles that the Lord Jesus performed (20:30–31). *Seven such signs* are described in the book, all of them concerning Christ's ministry to the world. These are (1) turning the water into wine (chapter 2); (2) healing of the nobleman's son (chapter 4); (3) healing of the helpless man (chapter 5); (4) feeding of the five thousand (chapter 6); (5) walking on the water (chapter 6); (6) healing of the man born blind (chapter 9); and (7) raising of Lazarus from the dead (chapter 11).

All of these signs show that Jesus is the promised Messiah, the Son of God. In addition to the seven signs, there are *seven distinct sayings* of the Lord Jesus containing the words *I am*, followed by a predicate. These are (1) "I am the bread of life" (6:35); (2) "I am the light of the world" (8:12); (3) "I am the door" (10:9); (4) "I am the good shepherd" (10:11); (5) "I am the resurrection, and the life" (11:25); (6) "I am the way, the truth, and the life" (14:6); and (7) "I am the true vine" (15:1).

The Use of Key Words

Everything in the Gospel of John contributes to the purpose (20:30–31). John makes use of key words, the repetition of which impresses the reader with the writer's singleness of purpose. The two most significant of these are *life* and *believe*. Throughout the gospel we see opposite reactions to the Lord Jesus among various individuals and groups—rejection and reception, belief and unbelief.

1. Prologue: the Eternal Word (1:1–18)

The opening verses of John are usually called *the Prologue* (1:1–18). Thoughts introduced here are developed throughout the book. Some of the deepest truths concerning the person of the Lord Jesus Christ are found in these verses. His deity is taught (1:1). As God, he always existed (1:1–2), is the creator of all things (1:3), and is the source of all life (1:4). The truth known as *the incarnation* is described in 1:14. Along with the absolute deity of Jesus Christ stands the clear proclamation of his true and perfect humanity: "the Word became flesh" (1:14 ASV).

2. Christ's Ministry to the World (1:19–12:50)

When John the Baptizer proclaimed the Lord Jesus as the "Lamb of God" (1:29), he was referring to the Old Testament sacrifices and pointing forward to the cross. The testimony of John the Baptizer caused some to follow the Lord. These early disciples came to Christ in different ways, but most of them through the testimony or invitation of a friend or relative.

In the first miracle or sign at the wedding at Cana of Galilee, the Lord Jesus showed himself to have transforming power over nature. He "manifested forth his glory" (2:11).

When he was in Jerusalem for the Passover, a religious leader named Nicodemus came to see him at night. There is no record that Nicodemus asked a question at the beginning of the interview, but the Lord Jesus, who knows men's hearts (2:25), answered the question for which Nicodemus really wanted an answer (3:3). Natural birth cannot give a person a right standing before God. There must be an entirely new relationship, a birth from above (compare 2 Corinthians 5:17; 1 Peter 1:23; 1 John 5: 1; Titus 3:4–7). This supernatural work of the Holy Spirit of God (3:8) takes place when a person believes in the Lord Jesus Christ. One of the characteristic features of the gospel of John is the interviews the Lord Jesus had with various individuals.

The gospel of Christ is the triumph of eternal life over death. It is also the triumph of spiritual light over darkness. The Lord Jesus Christ is the light (1:4–5, 7–9; 8:12; 9:5). Every statement of the Lord provokes controversy because sin cannot abide holiness, or darkness light. We see in the gospel a rising tide of opposition to the Lord Jesus, induced especially by the religious leaders of the time. They recognized that he was claiming to be God, and they accused him of blasphemy and sought to put him to death (8:58–59; 10:33).

After the raising of Lazarus from the dead (chapter 11), the enemies of Christ begin to plot to put him to death (11:53). As he entered Jerusalem, offering himself to the nation of Israel as their King (12:12–19), the hour for which he had come into the world was fast approaching. As this section of the gospel concerning the public ministry of Christ closes, tension is high, with belief and unbelief in deadly combat.

3. Christ's Ministry to His Own (13:1–17:26)

On the night before his death, as he met privately with his disciples, the Lord Jesus spoke to them in what is called the *Upper Room Discourse* (chapters 13–16). He foretold his betrayal and denial, gave to his disciples a new commandment (13:34), and promised that the Holy Spirit would come to dwell in the believers (14:17).

In the upper room the Lord Jesus gave the beginning of doctrinal truths that are developed in the Epistles. The teaching concerning the distinctive ministries of the Holy Spirit in this age begins here. The Holy Spirit was to be "another Comforter" (14:16), just as the Lord Jesus himself had been.

Some have compared the public ministry of Christ to the court of the tabernacle in Old Testament times. If we follow this analogy, his private ministry to his own would correspond to the first room of the tabernacle, the Holy Place. In the tabernacle there was yet one more room, the Holy of Holies. This is represented in the gospel by the Lord's prayer of intercession (chapter 17).

It is marvelous that God would permit us to hear a conversation between the persons of the Godhead concerning us. This prayer is a pattern of the Lord's continuous intercession for all believers. He prays for our safekeeping, sanctification, unity, and glorification. This prayer anticipates the redeeming work of the Lord Jesus Christ upon the cross, the finished work by which he "obtained eternal redemption for us" (Hebrews 9:12).

4. Christ's Death and Resurrection (18:1–20:31)

John very explicitly shows the fulfillment of Old Testament Scripture in the death of the Lord Jesus Christ. Four times in the crucifixion account he calls attention to the fulfillment of specific passages (19:24, 28, 36–37).

The Lord Jesus had said that he had power to lay down his life and power to take it again (10:18). His taking it again in resurrection is the proof that all his claims were true. John does not list all the appearances of the Lord Jesus after his resurrection. His account must be studied in connection with the other gospels.

On the occasion of his second appearance to the apostles, his word to Thomas with Thomas' confession of faith—introduces the statement of the purpose of the book (20:29–31). Life, eternal life, comes through believing on the Lord Jesus Christ, the Son of God.

5. Epilogue: the Risen Lord (21:1–25)

On the wonderful occasion described in the closing chapter, the risen Lord shows himself to be the absolute master of our service. Early in his ministry he had given to the disciples a miraculous catch of fish, to introduce his command that they were to follow him and become fishers of men (Luke 5: 1–11). Now, under new conditions, he teaches them this lesson again, showing them that apart from him they cannot be successful, but that, following his direction, the result will be more than satisfactory.

At this unusual breakfast on the shore of the Sea of Tiberias, the Lord Jesus conducts the last interview in the book, an interview with Simon Peter. Graciously giving Peter opportunity to reaffirm his love three times, after his threefold denial, he then shows Peter his personal responsibility, saying, "Follow me."

The Lord Jesus Christ, the eternal Word made flesh, the worker of the mighty signs, the speaker of the *I am* sayings, the crucified one risen gloriously from the dead is the sovereign master of our lives. So the gospel of John concludes: "If I will . . . follow me" (21:22–23).

ACTS

The book called *The Acts of the Apostles was* written by Luke as a sequel to the gospel bearing his name (Acts 1:1–2). The gospel record told "all that Jesus began both to do and teach. "The record in Acts tells what the Lord Jesus continued to do and teach after his ascension. Consequently, the book might well be called *The Acts of the Risen Christ by the Holy*

Spirit through the Disciples. The events recorded cover more than thirty years, from the ascension of the Lord Jesus Christ until the end of the second year of Paul's first Roman imprisonment (probably the spring of A.D. 63). The book shows the spread of the Gospel, following the pattern laid out by the Lord Jesus himself in his closing message to the apostles: "But you shall receive power, after that the Holy Spirit is come upon you: and you shall be witnesses unto me both in Jerusalem, and in all Judea, and in Samaria, and unto the uttermost part of the earth" (Acts 1:8). The book has two main divisions:

1. WITNESSING IN JERUSALEM, JUDEA, AND SAMARIA (chapters 1–1 2)

2. WITNESSING UNTO THE UTTERMOST PART OF THE EARTH (chapters 13–28)

In the first division, the apostle Peter is the leading character; in the second division, it is the apostle Paul.

1. Witnessing in Jerusalem, Judea, and Samaria (chapters 1–12)

Waiting in Jerusalem until the enduement of power from the Holy Spirit as the Lord Jesus had commanded, the apostles and other believers numbering "about an hundred and twenty" (1:15) chose Matthias to take the place of Judas Iscariot. On the Day of Pentecost (2:1) the Holy Spirit came in the sense that he began new ministries. This was the fulfillment of the promises made by John the Baptizer and the Lord Jesus himself (Acts 1:5) concerning the baptism of the Holy Spirit, that ministry by which the Spirit of God united all believers into the body of Christ (see 1 Corinthians 12:13). Before Pentecost there were individual believers; after Pentecost, the church.

30

As the apostles preached in Jerusalem and performed miracles in the power of the Holy Spirit, many were added to the church (2:47). Opposition soon arose and became intensified and persecution followed.

One uniqueness of Acts is the inclusion of sermons and addresses. There are at least seventeen of these and references to a number of others. Eight are by Peter, one is by James, one by Stephen, and seven by Paul.

Throughout these early chapters we see the boldness of Peter, John, and other believers in testifying of their risen Lord. The doctrine of the resurrection of Christ is prominent throughout the book, since it is a necessary part of the Gospel. Although forbidden to preach Christ, the apostles took their stand saying: "We cannot but speak the things which we have seen and heard" (4:20); "We ought to obey God rather than men" (5:29).

Along with persecution from the religious leaders came internal trouble. The sin of Ananias and Sapphira, comparable in some respects to the sin of Achan in the nation of Israel (Joshua 7), was judged by God not only as a punishment upon the individuals but as a deterrent to others who might contemplate similar sin. Dissension among the believers concerning the distribution of material aid led to the appointment of men to oversee this part of the work. Although the word *deacon* is not used in the text, it seems evident that this was the beginning of the office of deacon in the church. Among the seven deacons chosen, Stephen and Philip were outstanding. The former, who became the first martyr for Christ, in a wonderful address before the council, sketched the history of God's people in Old Testament times and accused the nation of Israel of persecuting the prophets and of murdering the Lord Jesus Christ. It is upon the occasion of Stephen's death by stoning that Saul, who is to become so prominent in the book, is first introduced (7:58).

Up to this time, the preaching had been in the city of Jerusalem. After the death of Stephen, persecution caused believers to scatter throughout Judea and Samaria, thus fulfilling the purpose of the Lord Jesus. Philip, the deacon, became the evangelist to the Samaritans (8:5–25) and the bearer of the Gospel to the Ethiopian treasurer (8:26–40).

One of the most remarkable and far-reaching events in the book and in all history was the conversion of Saul of Tarsus, described in chapter 9 and again in his own words twice more, in chapters 22 and 26. The transformation of Saul from the chief persecutor of Christians to the chief missionary of the Gospel is an event that cannot be explained naturally. Only the power of God can account for it. (For supplementary material on the early years after Saul's conversion read Galatians 1–2.)

After the accounts of the conversion of Saul, his preaching in Damascus, his first visit to Jerusalem after his conversion, and his return to his native city of Tarsus, the record returns to the ministry of Peter, the great apostle to the Jews. However, in keeping with the promise of the Lord Jesus that he would give to Peter the keys of the kingdom of heaven (Matthew 16:19), Peter becomes the instrument of God in opening the door of faith to the Gentiles, as he had been in opening the door of faith to the Jews (Acts 2). The conversion of Cornelius (Acts 10) marks a great turning point in the book and in the history of the church. From here on it is clear that the Gospel is for Gentiles as well as Jews. As Peter described and vindicated his ministry to Cornelius (11:1–18), the believers said, "Then God has also granted to the Gentiles repentance to life" (NKJV).

Acts 11:19–20 introduces Antioch, the place where the disciples were first called Christians (11:26) and from which Paul began his great missionary journeys. This division closes with the persecution brought on by Herod Agrippa I, in which James, the son of Zebedee, was killed (12:2). Peter was imprisoned and miraculously delivered, and Herod himself was judged by God.

2. Witnessing unto the Uttermost Part of the Earth (chapters 13–28)

In chapter 13, Saul of Tarsus is first introduced as Paul, his Roman name. It is probable that he carried both names from birth. As he began his ministry among the Gentiles, he used his Gentile name rather than his Hebrew name since, although he was a Jew, he was also a Roman citizen.

In the second division of the book of Acts *three great missionary journeys* of the apostle Paul are described, as well as his voyage to Rome near the close of the book. On the *first missionary journey* (chapters 13–14) Barnabas and Paul are sent off by the Holy Spirit and by the church at Antioch to carry the Gospel into regions where it had not been heard. On this journey they visited the island of Cyprus and landed on the southern coast of Asia Minor, going to Perga and then preaching the Gospel in Antioch of Pisidia, in Iconium, Lystra, and Derbe. Following the principle of taking the Gospel first to the Jew (compare Romans 1:16), they preached in the synagogue. When the Jews refused the Gospel, they turned to the Gentiles (compare 13:46). At Lystra, Paul was stoned and left for dead, but God had yet a much greater ministry for him (14:19–20). At the close of this journey Paul and Barnabas returned to Antioch in Syria (14:26), which is the center of action in this division of the book, as Jerusalem is in the first.

The teaching that one must become a Jew in order to become a Christian, troubled the Gentile converts and led to the calling of a conference in Jerusalem which Paul and Barnabas attended. There the apostles and leading men of the church came to a unanimous decision that God was taking out from among the Gentiles a people for his name (15:14) and that Gentiles did not need to become Jews in order to be Christians. This was not a dispute among the apostles; nor were they divided in any way; but Peter, James, Paul, and all the others were in agreement against the Judaizers. Paul refers to these same Judaizers in several of his epistles, particularly in Galatians, where he sounds this same note of Christian liberty from the law which we find in the words of James at the council of Jerusalem.

On the *second missionary journey* (15:40 ff.) Paul is accompanied by Silas. He revisits churches that he had founded on the first journey and at one of them, evidently at Lystra, he finds a young believer named Timothy (16:1), who accompanies him and who has a prominent part in the later history. On this journey the Gospel first goes to Europe as Paul responds to the vision of the man of Macedonia (16:9). At this point also, the writer, Luke, first joins Paul's company, as indicated by the pronoun *we* in 16:10. On this journey Paul founded churches at Philippi in Macedonia (chapter 16), at Thessalonica (17:1–9), at Berea (17:10–14). At Athens, on Mars' Hill, where the philosophers customarily spoke, Paul boldly announced the resurrection of the Lord Jesus (17:15–32).

From Athens he went to Corinth. There he remained about a year and a half. This second journey ends in Syria (18:18).

On the *third missionary journey* Paul spent almost three years in the great city of Ephesus in the Roman province of Asia. Leaving Ephesus after a tumultuous riot, he revisits Macedonia and Greece; then returning to Asia, he holds a solemn farewell with the Ephesian elders whom he meets at Miletus (20:17–38).

Paul did not return to Antioch from this third journey; for in the city of Jerusalem, where he had gone bearing the generous collection for the saints from the Gentile churches, he was arrested and almost lost his life. Addressing the multitude (chapter 22), and later the Jewish council (chapter 23), Paul is rescued from death through Roman intervention and taken to Caesarea, the seat of the Roman governor, Felix. He continues as a prisoner in Caesarea for two years (24:27). Later, before Festus, Felix' successor as governor, he appeals to Caesar (25:10–11).

In his impressive defense before King Agrippa (Herod Agrippa II) Paul recounts for the last time in this book the story of his conversion. His whole life can be summed up in these words to the king, "I was not disobedient unto the heavenly vision" (26:19).

It was in the purpose of God that Paul should preach the Gospel in Rome. Although he did not go as he had planned, God took him there—as a prisoner. Through the stress of the shipwreck (chapter 27) and the dangers on the island of Melita (Malta), after many years of serving Christ and enduring many hardships, Paul came to the city of Rome. The book of Acts closes there, not because Paul's ministry was finished or because the history of the church was complete, but because Rome as the great capital of the empire represented the spread of the Gospel to the uttermost part of the earth.

2

The Letters of Paul

Thirteen books of the New Testament were written by the apostle Paul, whose ministry is described at length in the second half of the book of Acts. The letters of Paul, the apostle to the Gentiles (Romans 11:13; 15:16), fall into four groups: (1) those written during the second missionary journey, about A.D. 52 (1 and 2 Thessalonians); (2) those written during the third missionary journey, about 57 and 58 (1 and 2 Corinthians, Romans, and Galatians); (3) those written during the first Roman imprisonment, about 62 and 63 (Ephesians, Colossians, Philemon, and Philippians); (4) those written just prior to and during the second Roman imprisonment, 66–68 (1 Timothy, Titus, and 2 Timothy).

The main subject of the letters in group one is the return of the Lord. Those in group two pertain to the Gospel and its application in everyday life. The third group, usually called the *Prison Letters,* deals with truth concerning the church, the body of Christ. Group four, the *Pastoral Letters,* gives instruction for Christian ministry.

ROMANS

As we have seen, Romans was not the earliest of Paul's letters; but it was placed first in the collection of his writings because of its major importance. It was addressed to the saints at Rome (1:1–15) but is intended for all men, both Jews and Gentiles (2:1, 3, 17; 11: 13). It was written from Corinth, probably in the year 58.

The Gospels give the record of Christ's earthly ministry, his death, and resurrection, but do not explain doctrinal truth to any extent. The book of Acts continues the history, showing the preaching of the early Church concerning the death and resurrection of Christ, but gives little systematic explanation of the Gospel. Romans gives a systematic presentation of the work of Christ. It is foundational to other Pauline letters. Paul had a desire to set forth the Gospel in writing (1:1–4) and to preach at Rome, the capital of the empire (1:10, 15).

The theme of the epistle is "the Gospel of God" (1:1, 16; 15:16). The Gospel, or good news, is from God, and it concerns his Son, Jesus Christ. This Gospel includes the gift of imputed righteousness—"the righteousness of God"—which is emphasized more than sixty times in the epistle.

Outline of the Book

Romans is made up of an introduction, five main divisions, and a conclusion:

   1. INTRODUCTION: THE GOSPEL OF GOD (1:1–17)

   2. UNIVERSAL SINFULNESS (1:18–3:20)

3. JUSTIFICATION BY FAITH (3:21–5:21)

4. SANCTIFICATION (6:1–8:39)

5. GOD'S DEALINGS WITH ISRAEL (9:1–11:36)

6. OUR REASONABLE SERVICE (12:1–15:13)

7. CONCLUSION: PERSONAL TESTIMONY AND GREETINGS (15:14–16:27)

1. Introduction: the Gospel of God (1:1–17)

The introduction contains the salutation (1:17), expresses Paul's desire to go to Rome (1:8–15), and sets forth the theme of the epistle (1:16–17): "For I am not ashamed of the gospel of Christ: for it is the power of God unto salvation to every one that believes; to the Jew first, and also to the Greek. For therein is the righteousness of God revealed from faith to faith: as it is written, The just shall live by faith." This good news from God about the Lord Jesus Christ reveals a righteousness from God which is on the basis of faith and is received by faith. The quotation, which is from Habakkuk 2:4, is similarly used in two other New Testament letters (Galatians 3:11; Hebrews 10:38).

2. Universal Sinfulness (1:18–3:20)

Romans gives a logical and systematic presentation of the Gospel. In the first main division the need for the Gospel is seen in the universal sinfulness of mankind. Here we read that there is no righteousness in us. Both Jews and Gentiles "are all under sin" (3:9). "There is none righteous, no, not one" (3:10). "Every mouth" is "stopped"; no flesh is justified (3:19–20).

3. Justification by Faith (3:21–5:21)

Because we have no righteousness of our own, God provided righteousness through his Son, the Lord Jesus Christ. This righteousness is received by faith: "for all have sinned, and come short of the glory of God; being justified freely by his grace through the redemption that is in Christ Jesus" (3:23–24). This justification is by faith apart from human works (4:1–8), apart from ordinances (4:9–12), and apart from the law (4:13–25). Its results are seen in 5:1–11, and the section concludes with a comparison and contrast between Adam and Christ. Through Adam came sin, death, and condemnation. Through the Lord Jesus Christ came righteousness, life, and justification (5:12–21).

4. Sanctification (6:1–8:39)

The believer is identified with the Lord Jesus Christ in his death and resurrection (6:1–13). This leads to deliverance from the law (6:14–7:14); but because he has an old nature as well as a new nature, the believer finds himself doing what he does not want to do and unable to do what he wants to do (7:15–25). Deliverance can come only through the Lord Jesus Christ. The indwelling Holy Spirit frees us from the principle of sin and death and makes it possible for us to live a life pleasing to God (8:1–4). This section reaches a marvelous climax in Paul's confident assertion that all things work together for good to them that love God (8:28) and in his description of the security that we have in Christ.

5. God's Dealings with Israel (9:1–11:36)

In this division Paul answers the question as to why Israel has been set aside. God is sovereign in exercising his mercy (chapter 9). Israel had a responsibility toward God and failed (10:2–3), but God has not cast Israel away forever (11:1).

There is still a remnant that believes (11:5). Gentiles are warned to learn from Israel's experience (11:13–22), and the nation of Israel is yet to be saved (11:25–27). The section closes with a great doxology (11:33–36).

6. Our Reasonable Service (12:1–15:13)

The last main division shows how the righteousness that God produces in our lives is to go through us to others. Our responsibility as believers is shown toward God (12:1–2), toward fellow believers (12:3–16), toward all men (12:17–21), and toward government (13:1–7). The outworking of the law of love is seen in daily living (13:8–15:3). Jew and Gentile are seen to be one in Christ (15:4–13).

7. Conclusion: Personal Testimony and Greetings (15:14–16:27)

The apostle again expresses an earnest desire to minister to the saints in Rome: "that I may come unto you with joy by the will of God, and may with you be refreshed" (15:32). The list of those to whom he sends greetings (chapter 16) shows that he already had many friends and acquaintances there.

GALATIANS

Galatians belongs to the same chronological group of Paul's letters as Romans. Both Romans and Galatians have as their theme the *Gospel* , with its great truth of *justification by faith.* Romans presents the theme systematically. Galatians presents it polemically. That is, in Romans Paul defines and describes the Gospel. In Galatians he defends it against error.

There is difference of opinion among Bible scholars about the location of the churches of Galatia. Those who hold the South Galatian theory believe that these churches were at

Iconium, Lystra, and Derbe, cities first visited by Paul on his first missionary journey (Acts 14) and revisited on the second journey (Acts 16:1–5). Advocates of the North Galatian theory believe that the churches of Galatia were in the region first visited by Paul on his second missionary journey (Acts 16:6). The original destination is not essential to its message.

Galatians is primarily the letter of Christian liberty, for in it we see salvation by grace through faith apart from works and apart from the law. The epistle was written to refute the false teaching of the Judaizers (compare Acts 15), who tried to teach the Galatian Christians that they had to become Jewish proselytes in order to be saved.

The epistle is in three main divisions:

1. PAUL'S DEFENSE OF HIS APOSTOLIC AUTHORITY (chapters 1–2)

2. PAUL'S EXPLANATION OF THE GOSPEL (chapters 3–4)

3. PAUL'S APPLICATION OF THE GOSPEL TO CHRISTIAN LIVING (chapters 5–6)

Three words are used to characterize these divisions: (1) *personal;* (2) *doctrinal;* and (3) *practical.*

Since the Judaizers maintained that Paul was not truly an apostle, Paul had to defend his apostolic authority to substantiate his message. He asserts that he received the Gospel as a direct revelation from the Lord Jesus Christ (1:11–12) and cites various circumstances of his life to show his true apostleship.

In the second division of the epistle he shows that Abraham was justified by faith and that all who believe are spiritually the children of Abraham. Those who wish to be under the law are under the curse of God because they cannot keep the law (3:10–12), but Christ has redeemed us from the curse of the law by his death upon the cross (3:13). The true purpose of the law is to show men their need of the Savior (3:24). Those who believe in the Lord Jesus Christ are sons of God (3:26; 4:5).

In the final division of the epistle Paul shows that even as justification is by faith, so the Christian life with its progressive sanctification is also by faith. "If we live in the Spirit, let us also walk in the Spirit" (5:25). The flesh, or sinful nature, can do only evil works; but as the believer yields himself to the Spirit of God, the fruit of the Spirit is produced in his life (5:22–23). Hence, the Christian has nothing in himself of which to glory, but glories in the cross of Christ (6:14).

CORINTHIAN LETTERS

The founding of the church at Corinth is described in Acts 18. Paul first visited Corinth on his second missionary journey. It was a large city on the isthmus connecting northern and southern Greece, the capital of the Roman province of Achaia. It was an important commercial and shipping center and was notorious even among the pagan Greeks for its low moral standards. The verb *to Corinthianize* meant in the Greek language to live a licentious life.

First and Second Corinthians give us a more detailed picture of the life of a local church in Paul's day than do any of the other letters. These two Corinthian letters belong in the same chronological group as Romans and Galatians, since they were written on Paul's third missionary journey.

1 CORINTHIANS

First Corinthians was written from Ephesus, probably in the spring of A.D. 57 (1 Corinthians 16:8). The apostle had heard disturbing reports concerning conditions in Corinth and had also received a letter from the Corinthian church with inquiries concerning a number of subjects. The contents of 1 Corinthians are quite varied, dealing with many practical matters of Christian living and showing the effect of the Gospel on life. There is an extended treatment of the doctrine of the resurrection (chapter 15).

First Corinthians is essentially a letter of correction. Paul rebuked the Corinthian believers for their divisions, their condoning of immorality, their lawsuits against one another, their abuse of the Lord's Supper, and their disorder in the church generally.

The letter is in two main divisions:

1. CORRECTION OF CONDITIONS THAT HAD BEEN REPORTED TO PAUL BY THE HOUSEHOLD OF CHLOE AND OTHERS (chapters 1–6)

2. REPLY TO THE LETTER WHICH THE CORINTHIANS HAD WRITTEN TO PAUL (chapters 7–16)

1. Correction of Conditions That Had Been Reported to Paul by the Household of Chloe and Others (chapters 1–6)

The Corinthian church had received many spiritual gifts from God (1:7), but this did not insure the spirituality of the believers. Reports concerning factions and quarreling within the church troubled Paul, and he set about to correct this condition (1:1–11). The cause of this party spirit seems to have been an undue reliance upon "the wisdom of this world" (2:6), rather than upon the true wisdom of God. The wisdom of this world creates and fosters pride and self-centeredness in those who hold it, and this makes for division.

The wisdom of God contained in the Holy Scriptures is received differently by different kinds of men. The person who has not been born again through faith in the Lord Jesus Christ cannot receive it at all (2:14). A believer in Christ who has yielded to the Holy Spirit of God is capable of discerning all things (2:15). In between these two is a believer in Christ who is not yielded to God and who has not grown spiritually (3:1–4).

The Corinthian believers were in the latter category. They were permitting their old nature to dominate their lives. Hence, there were continued divisions among them. Paul shows that the Lord Jesus Christ is the foundation (3:11), that it is possible to build on this foundation either that which is lasting ("gold, silver, precious stones") or that which will be destroyed at the judgment seat of Christ ("wood, hay, stubble").

Faithfulness is necessary since we are God's stewards (4:1–2). Unless there is a change in this condition in Corinth, it will be necessary for the apostle to deal with it severely when he comes among them again (4:18–21).

Not only were there divisions in the Corinthian church, but there was also a lack of church discipline. A flagrant example of this was their failure to excommunicate a man who claimed to be a believer and yet persisted in gross immorality. Paul commanded them to put him out of the church (chapter 5).

Another example of their lack of discipline was their going to law before the pagan courts rather than settling their differences and disputes among themselves (6:1–8). This section of the epistle closes with a reminder of the sanctity of the body—in contrast to those immoral conditions which were common in the city of Corinth—and a reminder that believers are not their own but have been bought with a price (6:19–20).

2. Reply to the Letter that the Corinthians had Written to Paul (chapters 7–16)

The second main division of the epistle first takes up the subject of *marriage and divorce.* The apostle deals frankly with the responsibilities of husbands and wives to each other in the marriage relationship. (This passage should be compared with Ephesians 5:22–33.) The second subject discussed is the *eating of meat offered to idols* (chapters 8–10). Although this particular problem affects few Christians today, it illustrates the principles of Christian liberty and of self-limitation for the sake of the Lord Jesus Christ and of others. Paul speaks of his own liberty and of his use of that liberty for the good of others (chapter 9). He warns believers not to follow the sad example of Israel (10:1–12). The principles to be followed are set forth particularly at the close of the chapter (10:31–33).

The apostle next praises the Corinthians *for keeping the ordinances* that he had delivered to them (11:2), instructs them concerning *the place of women in the church* (11:13–16), and rebukes them for the *abuses of the Lord's Supper* (11:17–34). The expression at the beginning of chapter 12 ("now concerning") is the same in the original as in 7:1, 25; 8:1, and 16:1, showing that these are subjects about which the Corinthians had written to him.

The subject of *spiritual gifts* (chapters 12–14) is a difficult one and has been misunderstood by various groups of Christians throughout church history. Distinction must be made between spirituality and spiritual gifts. Spirituality is the condition of being filled with the Holy Spirit of God, that is, given over to his control (compare Ephesians 5:18). The spiritual gifts enable believers to perform certain acts or ministries. The Corinthian Christians are proof that spiritual gifts do not necessarily make the possessors morally or spiritually better. They abounded in spiritual gifts but were characterized by the apostle as "carnal" in their lives (3:1–4).

Since the church is the body of Christ, God has ordained that various members should have various gifts. Some of these gifts were of a temporary nature in the early church; others are to continue throughout the history of the church. All of them must be exercised in love (chapter 13), and all are for the edification of the body of Christ. If all who claim to have spiritual gifts would follow the regulations laid down by the apostle Paul in 1 Corinthians 14:23–40, there would be no problem.

Some of the Corinthians were denying the doctrine of *the resurrection of the body;* therefore, Paul showed that the resurrection of the Lord Jesus Christ is a part of the Gospel (15:3–4, 14, 17) and that Christ's resurrection is the guarantee of our resurrection.

The letter closes with instructions concerning the *collection for the saints* (16:1), a reference to Christian stewardship, which is developed more fully in the second letter.

2 CORINTHIANS

Second Corinthians was probably written in the autumn of 57 from somewhere in Macedonia, perhaps from Philippi Paul had heard of the reception of his first epistle from Titus when he returned from Corinth and met Paul in Macedonia. This is the most personal of Paul's letters in setting forth his feelings toward those to whom he ministers. The epistle is in three main divisions:

1. MISSIONARY PRINCIPLES AND PRACTICE OF THE APOSTLE PAUL (chapters 1–7)

2. CHRISTIAN STEWARDSHIP (chapters 8–9)

3. VINDICATION OF PAUL'S APOSTLESHIP AND MINISTRY (chapters 10–13)

The theme of the epistle might be described as the ministry of a true servant of Christ (see 4:5).

1. Missionary Principles and Practice of the Apostle Paul (chapters 1–7)

In the first main division, Paul describes his relationship to the Corinthian Church, showing that he has been consistent in all his dealings with them. He rejoices in the triumph that God gives in Christ (2:14) and describes the ministry of the new covenant in contrast to the old covenant of the law (3:6–18). The message is Christ (4:5). The chief motive is Christ's love (5:14). The object is to win men to him (5:20).

In 6:11–7:16, Paul expresses to the Corinthians his desire that their love for him will be equal to his love for them.

2. Christian Stewardship (chapters 8–9)

Enlarging upon what he said in 1 Corinthians 16 concerning the collection for the saints, Paul discusses Christian giving, using the example of Macedonian believers (8:1–8) and pointing to the supreme example, the Lord Jesus himself. "For you know the grace of our Lord Jesus Christ, that, though he was rich, yet for your sakes he became poor, that you through his poverty might be rich" (8:9). He exhorts the Corinthians to generosity and shows the blessings that follow it. In these two chapters are principles for all of us to follow in our stewardship of money.

3. Vindication of Paul's Apostleship and Ministry (chapters 10–13)

Although the Corinthian Church generally had received Paul's first letter in the right spirit, some were rebellious and denied Paul's apostolic authority. To such people Paul addresses the words in the third division of the epistle (chapters 10–13). He refutes the accusations that he was cowardly and weak (10:1–11) and reminds them that Corinth is within the sphere of his apostolic authority (10:12–18; compare Romans 15:20). Although he does not like to commend himself, he does so (chapters 11 and 12) because false teachers masquerading as apostles of Christ (11:13) are trying to rob them of their blessing. He shows his labors and his sufferings for the Lord Jesus Christ (11:16–33) and the visions and revelations that God has given him (12:1–10). His reason for describing these matters is his unfailing love for them (12:11–18). Paul mentions that he intends to visit them again (12:19–13:10), and closes with greetings and benediction (13:11–14).

George Herbert said of this letter: "What an admirable epistle the second to the Corinthians! How full of affection! He joys and he sorrows, he grieves and he glories. Never was there such care of a flock expressed save by the great Shepherd of the fold, who first shed tears over Jerusalem and afterward blood." Charles Hodge commented that if in Romans we see the mind of Paul, in 2 Corinthians we feel his heart.

3

The Prison Letters

The letters of Paul to the Ephesians, Colossians, Philippians, and to Philemon, are called the *Prison Letters* because they were written during Paul's first Roman imprisonment. It is likely that Paul arrived in the city of Rome in the spring of A.D. 61. According to Acts 28:30, he stayed "two whole years in his own hired house." This would bring him to the spring of 63. Probably he was released before the burning of Rome in 64. When he wrote Philippians, he was expecting to be released (Philippians 1:19–26), a hope to which he also refers in Philemon 22. Ephesians, Colossians, and Philemon were dispatched at the same time by the same messengers (Ephesians 6:21–22; Colossians 4:7–9; Philemon 12, 23–24). It is possible that these three letters were written in the year 62 and that the letter to the Philippians was written in the following year.

EPHESIANS

The church at Ephesus was blessed by the ministry of the apostle Paul for a comparatively long time during his third missionary journey (Acts 19:1–20:1, 31). The association with the Ephesian believers had been most intimate, as his address to the Ephesian elders at Miletus shows (Acts 20:17–38).

Ephesians and Colossians emphasize the truth of the church as the body of which Christ is the head. Paul had mentioned this same truth earlier in Romans 12 and 1 Corinthians 12, but he developed it more fully in these letters. Ephesians shows the believer seated with Christ in the heavenlies and exhorts him to live in accordance with this high calling.

Ephesians is in two main divisions of three chapters each:

1. THE BELIEVER'S POSITION IN CHRIST
   (chapters 1–3)

2. THE BELIEVER'S CONDUCT IN THE WORLD
   (chapters 4–6)

The content of Ephesians can be summarized by three words: *sitting, walking, standing.* The believer's position is described as being seated with Christ in the heavenlies (Ephesians 2:6). His responsibility is to walk in a manner that fits this calling (Ephesians 4:1). And he is to stand against the wiles of the devil (Ephesians 6:11).

1. The Believer's Position in Christ (chapters 1–3)

After the salutation (1:1–2) the believer is described as possessing all spiritual blessings (1:3–14). The work of all the persons of the Godhead is seen in that believers have been chosen by the Father (1:3–6), redeemed by the Son (1:7–12), and sealed by the Holy Spirit (1:13–14).

Ephesians contains two great prayers of Paul for the believers there. The first of these (1:15–23) is that they would fully experience the knowledge of what God has provided for them. At the close of the prayer he speaks of the church as the body of Christ (1:23).

The apostle then describes salvation by grace (2:1–10), referring to what we were in the past (2:1–3), what we are in the present (2:4–6), and what we will be in the future (2:7–10). This is followed by the development of the thought of the oneness of Jews and Gentiles in Christ (2:11–22), showing what the Gentiles were without Christ (2:11–12). The apostle then describes the one body, composed of both Jews and Gentiles (2:13–18), which he characterizes also as the one building (2:19–22), of which the Lord Jesus Christ is the chief cornerstone.

The opening part of chapter 3 sets forth a mystery (3:1–12). Paul had been made a minister of the dispensation of the grace of God (3:1–7), declaring that which previously had not been fully revealed, "that the Gentiles should be fellow-heirs, and of the same body, and partakers of his promise in Christ by the gospel" (3:6), and offering to man the fellowship of this mystery (3:8–12).

This leads to the second of Paul's great prayers (3:14–21)—that believers may "know the love of Christ, which passes knowledge" (3:19 NKJV). The prayer closes with a doxology confessing God's ability to exceed all our greatest expectations (3:20–21).

2. The Believer's Conduct in the World (chapters 4–6)

In the light of all that God has done for us, we are exhorted to walk in a way that is in keeping with his high calling. The term *walk* is used for the believer's life and conduct in the world. This walk is to be worthy (4:1–16), that is, in harmony with the position that we have in Christ. It is to be different (4:17–32). It is to be loving (5:1–14) and wise (5:15–6:9). This can be accomplished only through the power of the Holy Spirit (5:18), resulting in praise and thanksgiving

(5:19–20) and in the believer's submission in the practical relationships of life (5:21–6:9).

The Christian walk is also seen as a warfare (6:10–20). The believer can be strong, not in himself, but only in the Lord as he puts on the whole armor of God (6:10–17) and engages in prayer (6:18–20). The closing greetings (6:21–24) mention Tychicus, the bearer of the letter.

COLOSSIANS

As Romans and Galatians are companion letters concerning the truths of the Gospel, so Ephesians and Colossians are companion letters concerning the truths of the church as the body of Christ. Ephesians emphasizes the church—the body of which Christ is the head. Colossians, on the other hand, emphasizes Christ—the head of the body. Like Galatians, Colossians was written to combat error. The error in this case was a false teaching which later became known as Gnosticism. The adherents of this doctrine claimed a superior knowledge and denied the full deity and the true humanity of the Lord Jesus Christ. The Colossian believers are exhorted to repudiate such error and to "hold the head" (2:19); that is, have a true doctrine of Christ.

Like Ephesians, the Colossian letter combines doctrine and practice.

1. CHRIST, THE ALL-SUFFICIENT HEAD
   (chapters 1–2)

2. THE LIFE OF THE NEW MAN IN CHRIST
   (chapters 3–4)

After sending greetings (1:1–2), Paul thanks God for the Colossians (1:3–8), of whom he had heard through Epaphras, who had come to him in Rome. He prays for them in a prayer similar to his prayers in Ephesians (1:9–14).

This letter is remarkable for its description of the glories of the Lord Jesus Christ. His person is described (1:15–19) and his absolute deity insisted upon. His marvelous work is described (1:20 2:3)—that which he accomplished through his death on the cross and that which he works in those who believe.

The Colossians must be warned against false teachers (2:4–23). They must find that the Lord Jesus Christ alone is completely sufficient for them (2:10). They are to beware of philosophy and legalism and false asceticism.

The practical portion of the letter is like a condensation of Ephesians. The believer is to seek the things above. This involves putting to death sin (3:5), that is, putting off the old man (3:9) and putting on the new (3:10). All things are to be done "in the name of the Lord Jesus" (3:17). The instructions given are to specific groups of Christians, as in Ephesians.

The letter closes with indications of loving Christian fellowship in the mention of a number of friends. Tychicus is referred to as the bearer of this letter also (4:7) and Onesimus is mentioned (4:9), thus linking this letter with the one to Philemon.

PHILEMON

This brief letter is a personal note to Philemon, a Christian of Colosse, on behalf of Onesimus. The story seems to be this: Onesimus, a slave of Philemon, ran away and perhaps took some of Philemon's property with him. He wandered to Rome, where he came in contact with Paul and was saved. Paul then sent him back to Philemon with this letter.

Beginning with greetings and thanksgiving for Philemon, Paul proceeds to intercede for Onesimus. He could have asserted his apostolic authority, but he preferred to emphasize love, not necessity. Philemon owed much to Paul. Here was an opportunity for him to repay Paul by the way he treated Onesimus.

This little letter is a wonderful illustration of the doctrine of imputation: "If you count me therefore a partner, receive him as myself. If he has wronged you, or owes you anything, put that on my account" (verses 17–18). That which Paul pleads on behalf of Onesimus, the Lord Jesus Christ in full measure has done for us. Our sins were put to his account, and God now receives us as he receives his own Son.

PHILIPPIANS

The founding of the church at Philippi is described in Acts 16. The problems in this church seem to have been minor compared to those in some of the other churches. This brief letter describes the joyous Christian experience. The joy that Paul has does not flow from his circumstances (he was a prisoner), but from the Lord himself. After the salutation (1:1–2), Paul describes his attitude toward the Philippians, an attitude of thanksgiving, of prayer, and of desire to see them (1:3–11). He then tells of his own circumstances and of his attitude toward them (1:12–26) and exhorts the Philippians that their manner of life may befit the Gospel of Christ (1:27–30).

The apostle desires that the Philippians may have the mind of Christ (2:1–11). He expresses his concern for them (2:12–30). He finds his confidence in the Lord Jesus Christ (3:1–16). And he encourages the believers in their walk (3:17–21).

The closing exhortations (4:1–9) are to unity, to rejoicing, to moderation, and to quiet, prayerful dependence upon God. The apostle shows how God supplies (4:10–20), and closes with brief greetings from the believers in Rome (4:21–23).

Christ is beautifully portrayed throughout the letter. He is the believer's life (chapter 1), the believer's example (chapter 2), the object of the believer's faith and hope (chapter 3), the believer's strength (chapter 4).

All of the Prison Letters (the third chronological group of Paul's letters) deal with "church truth" and "Christian life truth." Merely to know their contents is insufficient. This knowledge must lead to personal appropriation and application, that Christ may indeed control our lives.

4

The First and Final Letters of Paul

1 THESSALONIANS

First Thessalonians is the earliest of Paul's inspired letters. The founding of the church in Thessalonica is described in the Acts 17:1–10. Apparently Paul was able to be with the church only a brief time, yet was able not only to give the Thessalonians the Gospel, but also to give much instruction concerning Christian living and much truth about the return of the Lord.

Later, from Corinth, after being rejoined by Timothy and Silas (3:2–6), Paul wrote to the new church to exhort and comfort them. It is likely that the Thessalonians had misunderstood some of Paul's teachings, particularly about the return of the Lord. They were troubled, not knowing the future of loved ones who had died since becoming believers.

This letter emphasizes the Lord's return (1:10; 2:19; 3:13; 4:13–18; 5:23). Its theme might be stated as *the believer's walk in view of the Lord's return.* Paul exhorts the believers to "walk worthy of God" (2:12; compare 3:12–13; 4:1, 12; 5:23). The life and character of the Thessalonian Christians is epitomized in 1:9–10: "[You] turned to God from idols to serve the living and true God; and to wait for his Son from heaven, whom he raised from the dead, even Jesus, which delivered us from the wrath to come."

The letter may be divided into three parts:

1. THE THESSALONIAN BELIEVERS AS EXAMPLES (1:1–10)

2. THE FAITHFUL MINISTRY OF PAUL (2:1–3:13)

3. EXHORTATION, INSTRUCTION, AND COMFORT (4:1–5:28)

Paul had no difficulty in finding things for which to thank God in regard to the Thessalonians (1:2–4). Not only had they become followers; they were also examples in their whole region.

Paul reminds them of his coming, of his arduous and blameless ministry, and of his continued compassion and concern for them. Even though they were an exemplary church, they needed exhortation concerning their manner of life and they needed instruction concerning believing loved ones who had died. This occasion gives rise to one of the central passages in the Scriptures on the rapture of the church (4:13–18). The truth of the coming of the Lord is always accompanied in Scripture by commands for godly living.

Because they were not in darkness, they could "watch and be sober" (5:6).

The letter shows the apostle's tender care and love for these new believers as a true pastor and as a father in the Lord (2:11).

2 THESSALONIANS

Second Thessalonians was probably written from Corinth soon after 1 Thessalonians. It corrects misunderstandings concerning "the day of the Lord" and rebukes errors in conduct among the Thessalonians. The Thessalonian Christians were in trouble and were being persecuted (1:4–7). False teachers had led them to wonder if "the day of the Lord" was already present. (It seems likely that the reading, "the day of the Lord," in 2:2 as found in the ASV is accurate, rather than "the day of Christ" as in the KJV.) Some of the Thessalonian Christians were neglecting the ordinary duties of life because they believed that they were in the end-time period. As someone has said, in the first letter believers are told to wait while working (1 Thessalonians 1:9–10); in the second, they are told to work while waiting (2 Thessalonians 3:3–13).

Dr. James M. Gray's comment is helpful: "Paul had taught the believers that before 'the day of the Lord' they would be caught up to meet Him in the air, to be forever with Him. But these false teachers sought to reverse this order and had them believe that 'the day of the Lord' had already come. If it had, and they had not been gathered unto Him, they had reason indeed to be troubled, for then their faith and hope were vain and Paul had deceived them. But the apostle offsets this false teaching, in the doing of which he reveals matters of deep interest concerning the apostasy."

In the opening chapter of the letter, the apostle speaks of the tribulation of the Thessalonian believers and reminds them of the righteous judgment of God that is coming upon the earth. The fact that God is sovereign in history is frequently cited in the Scriptures as reason for the believer's confidence and as a stabilizing factor in his life and testimony.

The Thessalonians are not to be deceived concerning "the day of the Lord." The "coming of our Lord Jesus Christ" and "our gathering together unto him" guarantee that we shall not go through the tribulation period of "the day of the Lord." The revelation of the "man of sin" (2:3) cannot take place until the restrainer is removed. (The word *let* in 2:7, KJV, is used in the older sense of *hinder* or *restrain.*) Since the restrainer is viewed as a person, he must be none other than the Holy Spirit of God himself, now working in and through the Church.

The closing chapter contains exhortations and warnings. The Thessalonian Christians are to withdraw from the disorderly (3:6), to follow Paul's example (3:7), to be industrious in daily work (3:10–12), to persevere in good deeds (3:13).

The closing salutation mentions the fact that Paul put his personal signature on every letter that he wrote, even though most of his letters were dictated by him to a secretary.

1 TIMOTHY

First Timothy is one of three short letters that are often called the *Pastoral Letters.* The other two are Titus and 2 Timothy. These letters contain instructions primarily for those who oversee churches, but every child of God can find instruction and blessing in them.

This letter is addressed to Timothy, who is first mentioned in Acts 16:1. He lived in Lystra, one of the cities that Paul visited twice on his first missionary journey (Acts 14:6–21). When Paul returned to Lystra on his second missionary journey, he decided to take Timothy with him as a companion and helper in his travels. From this time on, Timothy was intermittently with the apostle on his journeys. He is mentioned frequently in the New Testament.

It is likely that Paul was released from prison late in A.D. 63 or early in A.D. 64 (after the close of the book of Acts). During the next few years he probably traveled to various parts of the Roman Empire. This letter was probably written about the year A.D. 65, between Paul's first and second Roman imprisonments. Timothy had been left to serve in the church at Ephesus (1 Timothy 1:3). This letter was written to instruct him concerning problems he had to face as a spiritual leader in the church. He was still a relatively young man (1 Timothy 4:12) and seems by nature to have been rather timid and retiring (2 Timothy 1:6–8).

The theme of this letter might be expressed as *behavior in the household of God* (1 Timothy 3:15). It seems convenient to consider the letter in five parts:

1. SOUND DOCTRINE (chapter 1)

2. PRAYER AND WORSHIP (chapter 2)

3. CHURCH OFFICERS (chapter 3)

4. APOSTASY (chapter 4)

5. PASTORAL OVERSIGHT (chapters 5–6)

Timothy is commanded by Paul to resist false doctrine (1:3–4). He is reminded that the real purpose (or end) of doctrine is love (verse 5). The false teachers had missed this in their meaningless talk about the law (verse 6). Paul's salvation has special significance as a pattern or example for all men (verses 12–17). He was the chief of sinners, although by the standards of his contemporaries he was considered one of the best of men (Acts 23:1; 2 Timothy 1:3; Philippians 3:4–6). Because Paul was saved, we know that the worst man can be saved and the best man needs to be saved.

The instruction concerning prayer (chapter 2) primarily concerns public prayer and worship, and Paul gives it primary importance (verse 1). When Paul wrote this, the emperor was Nero, one of the worst of rulers; yet Paul said Christians were to pray for him (compare Romans 13:1–7; 1 Peter 2:13–17).

The list of qualifications for officers in the church (chapter 3) is not meant to be all inclusive, but certainly must be taken into account in any church that seeks to conform to the scriptural pattern. Many churches today are failing in their God-appointed responsibilities by not adhering to the principles laid down here.

Paul warns Timothy concerning the perils of the future (4:1–5) and exhorts him to set an example of godliness in view of the apostasy that is coming (verses 6–12). He is to give attention to three main tasks: the reading of the Scriptures, exhortation, and teaching (verses 13–16).

The pastoral oversight described in chapters 5 and 6 outlines the attitude of the pastor toward all types of people, gives personal instructions and warnings to Timothy, rebukes false teachers, and charges Timothy to "fight the good fight of faith" (6:12). It can be seen from 2 Timothy 4:7 that Paul heeded his own advice. It was because he lived a godly life himself that he could tell others how to live it. In the final charge to Timothy (6:20), one can hear the very heart cry of Paul in his desire that his "son in the faith" may receive the Lord's "well done."

2 TIMOTHY

Second Timothy was the last letter Paul wrote. He was again a prisoner, this time apparently in a dungeon in Rome, expecting soon to be executed (4:6). The letter was probably written in A.D. 68, the year of Paul's death. It describes the life and conduct of "a good soldier of Jesus Christ" (2:3). This conduct is to be exemplary (chapter 1), courageous (chapter 2), steadfast (chapter 3), and fervent (chapter 4).

Like 2 Peter and Jude, this letter warns of the apostasy that had begun to set in. The apostle is aware of those who have turned away from the truth (1:15; 4:10). He encourages and exhorts Timothy to not be ashamed of the testimony of Christ (1:8) and to hold fast sound teaching (1:13).

In the second chapter of the letter, Timothy, Paul's son in the faith, is exhorted to be a courageous soldier (verses 1–4), a careful athlete (verse 5), a persevering farmer (verse 6), a diligent workman (verse 15), a clean vessel (verses 20–21), and a gentle servant of the Lord (verses 24–26).

That which will sustain Timothy in the perilous time is his knowledge of the Word of God. He is exhorted to continue in the things he has learned (3:14), for "all scripture" is inspired of God, and is profitable in Christian living (3:16–17).

The solemn charge to Timothy in the concluding chapter becomes more poignant as we think of the life of the apostle Paul himself and hear his testimony as he approaches the goal: "I have fought a good fight, I have finished my course, I have kept the faith" (4:7). Now he looks forward to the Lord's heavenly kingdom (4:18).

TITUS

Titus is similar to First Timothy. Both were written about the same time to friends of the apostle who had the responsibility of pastoral oversight. Titus emphasizes the godly conduct of all believers. *Good works* is a key phrase (2:3, 5, 10, 14; 3:8, 14; compare also 1:16 and 3:1, 5), and the key passage is 2:11–14.

Titus, who is mentioned by Paul a number of times in his other letters, had been given the responsibility of ministering to the church on the island of Crete (1:5). It was essential that he uphold the standards of doctrine and practice in ordaining elders or bishops. The letter may be outlined as follows:

1. LEADERS IN THE LIFE OF A CONGREGATION (chapter 1)

2. PERSONAL LIVES OF MEMBERS OF THE CONGREGATION (chapters 2–3)

Along with the instructions concerning godly Christian living, there is the constant reminder of what God has done for us in making us his children. Faith in Christ and godly living go hand in hand: "This is a faithful saying, and these things I will that you affirm constantly, that they which have believed in God might be careful to maintain good works" (3:8).

Titus had a difficult task in Crete. The instructions given to him can be of great help and comfort to Christian workers today in similar surroundings.

5

The Letter to the Hebrews

Although some late manuscripts entitle this book *The Letter of Paul the Apostle to the Hebrews,* and though many Christians believe Paul wrote it, Paul's name does not appear in the letter itself. It is unlikely, therefore, that he wrote it, especially in view of the statement of the writer in 2:3. This verse seems to be quite contrary to Paul's statement about himself in Galatians 1:11–12. Dr. James M. Gray's comment is helpful: Hebrews "may have been written by Paul, or Apollos, or someone else; we cannot tell absolutely. . . . But while uncertainty exists as to the authorship of Hebrews, and also as to the location of those addressed, there can be no uncertainty as to the reason for writing the letter."

The book shows the superiority of the Lord Jesus Christ over Judaism. The introduction declares this (1:1–3). The Old Testament was given in many parts and many ways through prophets. The New Testament has been given through one who is the Son of God. The letter contains numerous quotations from the Old Testament and many allusions to the Mosaic system, including priesthood and ritual. It seems certain that the letter was written before the destruction of Jerusalem in A.D. 70 (note 10:11).

Two quotations from the Old Testament serve as the leading texts for the letter. These are "You are my Son" (Psalm 2:7) and "You are a priest forever after the order of Melchizedek" (Psalm 110:4). Keeping this in mind, we may outline the letter in this way:

1. INTRODUCTION: THE SUPERIORITY OF CHRIST (1:1–3)

2. THE SUPERIORITY OF THE PERSON OF CHRIST (1:4–4:13)

3. THE SUPERIORITY OF THE PRIESTHOOD OF CHRIST (4:14–10:18)

4. EXHORTATION TO FAITH, HOPE, AND LOVE (10:19–13:19)

5. CONCLUSION (13:20–25)

1. Introduction: The Superiority of Christ (1:1–3)

2. The Superiority of the Person of Christ (1:4–4:13)

In this section the Lord Jesus is seen to be better than angels, better than Moses. The Old Testament law had been given through the ministration of angels (2:2; compare Acts 7:53; Galatians 3:19).

Christ's superiority to angels is seen first of all in the fact that he is the Son of God. The quotations from the Old Testament bring out the contrast between him and the angels. They are "ministering spirits" (1:14) who worship him. He is the Son of God, the Lord.

At the beginning of chapter 2 we find the first of five warnings in the letter. The first one warns against neglect of the things which we have heard; the second, in chapters 3–4, warns against unbelief; the third, in chapter 6, against apostasy; the fourth, in chapter 10, against willful sin; the fifth, in chapter 12, against indifference. There is an urgency in all of these warnings, with a reminder of the certainty of judgment.

Following the first warning, we see the superiority of the Lord Jesus Christ to angels in that he is Son of Man, as well as Son of God. It is man to whom God has given the control of the earth. The Lord Jesus is the Son of Man, as prophesied in Psalm 8 (which is quoted here) and in other Old Testament passages. The Lord Jesus Christ became for a little while lower than the angels that he might bring those who have faith in him to a position above the angels. There is in this section an intimation of his high priesthood, a thought that is developed later in the letter.

Not only is the Lord Jesus Christ superior to angels, but he is superior to Moses, who was the mediator of the Old Covenant (3:13). No man was of greater importance to the people of Israel than Moses, the lawgiver. But Moses was a servant; Christ is the Son (verses 5–6).

The second warning is given against the sad background of Israel's unbelief in the wilderness, with extensive use of Psalm 95.

3. The Superiority of the Priesthood of Christ (4:14–10:18)

Having shown that Christ is greater and better in his *person* than the angels and Moses, the writer makes the transition to the *work of* Christ, particularly to his high priesthood (4:14–16). In his priestly work the Lord Jesus Christ is compared to Aaron, the first high priest of Israel, but is shown to be greater than Aaron because he belongs to a different order of priests, the order of Melchizedek (5:6 ASV). Melchizedek is mentioned in only two other places in the Bible. The historical account of the man is given in Genesis 14; the prophetic reference to Christ quoted in this passage in Hebrews is taken from Psalm 110.

Before the priesthood of Christ is developed, the third warning is given (chapter 6). The writer indicates that Melchizedek is a type, or divinely appointed prophetic symbol, of the Lord Jesus Christ. The typical teaching concerns not only what is said in Genesis 14, but also what is left unsaid. The name *Melchizedek* means "King of righteousness," and this is indeed the character of the Lord Jesus Christ. Melchizedek was king of Salem. This word means "peace."

The reference to Melchizedek here does not mean that the man was without father and mother; it means that the record tells us nothing about his ancestry. He suddenly appeared on the scene of history, and we are given no other information about him. Hence, he can be a suitable and fitting picture of the Lord Jesus Christ, who is the eternal, royal priest.

Christ's priesthood in contrast to the Levitical priesthood of Aaron is an eternal priesthood and he is both King and Priest, as Melchizedek was. This priesthood was confirmed with an oath. It is eternal, and the priest is not subject to death (7:24–25). This priesthood is superior in its place. This is a better ministry because it is heavenly; a better covenant, because it is eternal. There are better promises because they are spiritual.

Note the prominence of the word *better.* The better covenant (8:6) is the New Covenant, prophesied in the book of Jeremiah (Jeremiah 31:33). The covenant of the law, given through Moses, was intended to be temporary and preparatory to the Lord Jesus Christ. It contains external regulations and a ritualistic service. The New Covenant of the Lord Jesus

Christ affects individuals internally: "I will put my laws into their mind, and write them in their hearts" (8:10). While the nation of Israel, as such, will not enter into the New Covenant until the return of Christ, the believer in Christ receives the blessing of the New Covenant now.

The ritual and sacrifices of the Old Covenant were temporary and inadequate (9:8). Christ's sacrifice is better. It is complete and final. His death has confirmed the New Covenant (9:15). His work has been completed. He stands before God now, representing us as our intercessor, our advocate, and our forerunner. The Lord Jesus Christ is seen to be the fulfiller of the teaching of all of the major offerings of the book of Leviticus. The believer in Christ can now draw near to God. He does not have to come through human mediation, as the people of Israel did with the Levitical priesthood. The Israelite of old could not even enter the tabernacle. The believer in Christ has now entered into the holiest of all.

The fourth warning against willful sin (10:26–31) shows the impossibility of being saved in any other way than through the one complete, final sacrifice of the Lord Jesus Christ.

4. Exhortation to Faith, Hope, and Love (10:19–13:19)

The exhortation based upon Christ's person and Christ's priesthood actually begins at 10:19. Chapter 11, the great faith chapter, gives the roster of the heroes of faith in Old Testament times as a pattern and encouragement to us. The practical application of this is seen at the beginning of chapter 12. In the lives of these Old Testament people we see faith in action, faith that obeys God, faith that endures and does exploits.

The final warning in the letter concerns indifference. Esau is seen as an example of this. The writer not only encourages us to faith and hope, but also commands us to have love for our brethren (13:1). The exercise of love is seen in the practical relationships of life.

5. Conclusion (13:20–25)

The glorious letter, which presents our Lord Jesus Christ as our Great High Priest, needs to be applied to our own lives, that the benediction toward its close may be true of us: "Now the God of peace, that brought again from the dead our Lord Jesus, that great shepherd of the sheep, through the blood of the everlasting covenant, make you perfect in every good work to do his will, working in you that which is well-pleasing in his sight, through Jesus Christ; to whom be glory forever and ever. Amen" (13:20–21).

6

General Letters

James and 1 and 2 Peter are called *General Epistles,* or *Letters* because they are not addressed to one particular local church. James and 1 Peter have many similarities.

JAMES

This letter has been the occasion of much controversy, chiefly because it has been misunderstood.

The writer calls himself James, a servant of God and of the Lord Jesus Christ. He is undoubtedly James the Lord's brother, who was prominent in the council of Jerusalem, mentioned in Acts 15 (compare Matthew 13:55; Galatians 1:19; 2:9). During the Lord Jesus' earthly ministry he was not a believer (John 7:5), but the Lord appeared to him after his resurrection (1 Corinthians 15:7).

The letter is addressed to "the twelve tribes which are scattered abroad." It is clear from its contents, however, that it is not primarily addressed to Jews in general, but to Jewish Christians. It was evidently written quite early, perhaps as early as the year A.D. 50. It could not have been written, as some allege, to contradict the writings of Paul since it preceded them.

The letter bears similarities to the earthly teaching of the Lord Jesus and to the Old Testament wisdom teaching. It may be outlined as follows:

1. THE PROBLEM OF TESTING (1:1–18)

2. THE REALITY OF FAITH (1:19–2:26)

3. THE PROPER USE OF THE TONGUE (3:1–18)

4. ADMONITION AGAINST WORLDLY MINDED-
   NESS (4:1–5:6)

5. EXHORTATION AND COMFORT FOR THE
   OPPRESSED (5:7–20)

The portion of the letter which has been a stumbling block to many students of Scripture is the passage on faith and works (2:14–26). Some have supposed from this a conflict, as we have noted, between James and Paul; but the Scripture is everywhere in harmony with itself and, therefore, any interpretation of any part which seems to contradict another part must not be an accurate interpretation. The account of the Jerusalem council (Acts 15) shows that there was agreement among all the leaders in the church, including James and Paul. Actually, these two are in perfect agreement. Paul insists on faith that works through love (Galatians 5:6) and shows that good works are the product of faith (Ephesians 2:8–10). James, likewise, demands fruit as the proof of the reality of faith. (Compare the preaching of John the Baptizer in Matthew 3:8–9 and that of the Lord Jesus Christ himself in Matthew 7:20–21.) He shows that a so-called faith that does not result in works is like empty words of comfort to those who need not words but clothes and food. Sometimes that which calls itself faith is not faith at all. Abraham and Rahab are cited as examples of those who had real faith which manifested itself in action.

James brings to all of us a call for reality, "But be doers of the word, and not hearers only" (James 1:22).

His teaching concerning the tongue (chapter 3) is both practical and appropriate, for one cannot use the tongue properly apart from wisdom which God alone can give (1:5; 3:13–18).

James denounces the rich who are using their riches for the oppression and affliction of their fellow men, and encourages believers to have hope and to manifest the spirit and practice of prayer in their lives as they look for the return of the Lord.

1 PETER

First Peter was written to "the strangers scattered throughout" certain provinces in Asia Minor. It would seem that he is addressing Jewish Christians as James was, but there are some indications in the letter that he is thinking of Gentile believers as well (note, for example, 4:3 which could hardly have applied to Jews). The letter was probably written about the year A.D. 60 from "Babylon" (5:13). There is difference of opinion among commentators as to whether this was the literal, ancient Babylon in Mesopotamia or whether Peter is using the term symbolically for the city of Rome.

The purpose of the letter is to encourage Christians in their suffering for Christ, to show them that in Christ there is victory over suffering. The word *suffering* is prominent in the letter; however, it is clear that the apostle is not thinking of all kinds of suffering but of that which results from a true testimony for the Lord. No doubt the believers to whom Peter wrote were enduring persecution for their faith in

Christ. Peter shows Christ as our example in suffering and
the ground of our hope for future glory.

Although these distinctions should not be pressed too far,
Peter is characteristically the apostle of hope as Paul was of
faith and John was of love. He refers to the two main lines
of Old Testament prophecy concerning Christ, "the sufferings of Christ, and the glory that should follow" (1:11), and
looks through our suffering to our future hope. The letter
may be outlined as follows:

1. A LIVING HOPE THAT WITHSTANDS THE FIERY
   TRIAL (1:1–2:8)

2. THE CONDUCT OF THE HOLY AND ROYAL
   PRIESTHOOD (2:9–4:19)

3. SERVICE FOR THE CHIEF SHEPHERD (5:1–14)

1. A Living Hope that Withstands the Fiery Trial (1:1–2:8)

Peter shows that salvation includes the future aspect as well
as the past and the present. The believer in Christ is kept for
this future aspect of salvation and his inheritance is kept for
him. Because he knows this, he is equipped to withstand
testings. Hope, in Scripture, is not a vague wish of something
in the future, but an absolute certainty of future good.
Because we have been redeemed by the precious blood of
Christ (1:19), born again (1:23), made living stones in his
temple (2:5), we are able to live for him.

2. The Conduct of the Holy and Royal Priesthood (2:9–4:19)

As Christ's chosen priesthood, we are to glorify him (2:9).
This involves holiness in our behavior and will subject us to
suffering for his sake (2:20). In this the Lord Jesus Christ

himself is our great example (2:21). He is never presented in the Scripture as an example for the unsaved. He must first be received as personal Savior. He is depicted as an example for those who are his children. (Compare Philippians 2:5–11.) The holy conduct of the believer in Christ includes submission to government, subjection of servants to their masters, the proper relationship of husbands and wives (3:1–7), and a recognition of Christ's sufferings in which we partake (4:13). This does not mean, of course, that we can share in the vicarious suffering of Christ for sin, but we share in his suffering as we bear his name and endure reproach because of our faith in him. "Yet if any man suffer as a Christian, let him not be ashamed; but let him glorify God on this behalf (4:16).

3. Service for the Chief Shepherd (5:1–14)

Peter did not claim unusual authority for himself, for he classified himself as an elder among elders (5:1). All who have responsibility in service for Christ are to look toward him as the Chief Shepherd (5:4). As the letter draws to a close, we see again the two lines of thought concentrating on suffering and glory: "But may the God of all grace, who called us to His eternal glory by Christ Jesus, after that you have suffered a while, perfect, establish, strengthen, and settle you" (5:10 NKJV).

2 PETER

Second Peter has been a disputed book, both in ancient and in modern times. Some have denied its genuineness. But since it claims to have been written by Simon Peter (1:1), the only alternative to accepting his authorship would be to reject the book as a forgery. No Christian would want to take such a position. This letter is addressed to the same people to whom 1 Peter was addressed (compare 2 Peter 3:1). It was perhaps written about the year A.D. 65, not long before Peter's death (compare 1:14 with John 21:18–19). Second Peter is often classified as one of the *eschatological letters* because of its references to the end times. Peter is vitally interested in the "entrance into the eternal kingdom of our Lord and Savior Jesus Christ" (1:11 ASV).

Second Peter, which is Peter's farewell letter, has much in common with 2 Timothy, the last of Paul's writings. Both apostles solemnly warn against false teachers and their corrupting doctrines, against the apostasy that is coming upon the church. Peter, indeed, in this letter, refers to the letters of Paul (3:15–16). He appeals to believers to be steadfast in the midst of corruption. Again, as in 1 Peter, there is mention of suffering followed by glory. It may be said in a general way that the first letter emphasizes suffering, while the second emphasizes glory. Second Peter may be divided in this way:

1. THINGS THAT PERTAIN TO LIFE AND GODLINESS (chapter 1)

2. WARNING AGAINST FALSE TEACHERS (chapter 2)

3. THE RETURN OF THE LORD AND THE DAY OF THE LORD (chapter 3)

1. Things That Pertain to Life and Godliness (chapter 1)

Peter exhorts believers to advance in the Christian life (1:3–11) and sets forth his aim in writing—a statement of the guarantee of the apostolic testimony and the confirmation of the prophetic Word. He shows that the prophecy of the Old Testament has been confirmed by its partial fulfillment, of which he himself has been an eyewitness (1:16).

2. Warning Against False Teachers (chapter 2)

The warning against false teachers is a solemn one to which all should give heed. It refers to God's judgments upon men in ancient times, in the Flood, in the overthrow of Sodom and Gomorrah, as well as his judgments upon the angels that sinned. Peter shows that judgment is coming upon those who lead others astray through their false teachings. These false teachers in the Church are like the false prophet, Balaam (2:15), who "loved the wages of unrighteousness."

3. The Return of the Lord and the Day of the Lord (chapter 3)

In our day, in which the doctrine of the return of the Lord is ridiculed by many, we need to consider again the statements of 1 Peter 3. The idea that things happen according to fixed laws and patterns without any intervention of God in the natural world is an example, God tells us, of willful ignorance; for men can know that at one time God brought the great devastating flood. This ancient judgment serves as a grim reminder of a future judgment by fire. In view of this, we believers should conduct ourselves in holiness and godliness as we look for the return of Christ (3:11–12).

The closing exhortation of the apostle is applicable to every child of God. It can be accomplished only as we use and obey the Word of God: "But grow in grace, and in the knowledge of our Lord and Savior Jesus Christ" (3:18).

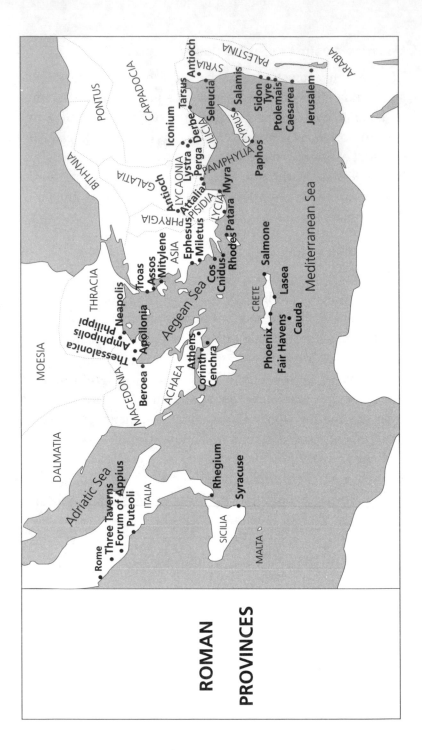

ROMAN PROVINCES

7

The Letters of John and Jude

1 JOHN

Although the writer of First John does not identify himself by name, it is clear, both from unbroken tradition in the early church and from the internal evidence in the letter itself, that it was written by the apostle John, the writer of the fourth gospel and the book of Revelation. The reference to Christ as the Word (1:1; compare John 1:1), the mention of the love of God toward us (4:9–10; compare John 3:16) and the statements concerning life as being connected with the Son (5:12; compare John 3:36) are only some of the internal evidences connecting this letter with the gospel of John.

This beautiful letter was addressed to believers in general (see 2:1, 12–14; 5:13). It was perhaps first circulated among the churches of Asia since John, in the later years of his life, seems to have ministered in Ephesus. It was probably written about the year A.D. 90, very late in John's life, perhaps about the same time as the Gospel of John and shortly before the book of Revelation.

The background and circumstances of the writing are not known definitely, but there seems to have been in the church a false teaching that later came to be known as Gnosticism. The Gnostics, who claimed to have superior knowledge (the term is taken from the Greek word for *know*), were of various types. Some of them denied the deity of the Lord Jesus Christ. Others denied his genuine humanity. The gospel of John and this letter combat both forms of Gnosticism. The gospel was written that men might be saved (John 20:30, 31); the letter, that believers may know that they are saved (1 John 5:13). The gospel, while recognizing the humanity of the Lord Jesus, emphasizes his deity (John 1:1; 20:30–31). The letter, while fully recognizing and stating his deity, emphasizes his true humanity (1 John 1:1–2; 4:2–3).

The letter, therefore, was written to give believers assurance of salvation (5:13) and to instruct them concerning their fellowship and joy in Christ (1:3–4).

The apostle's theme might be stated as "fellowship in the Father's family." The word *fellowship* is a sort of keynote (1:3) and emphasis is placed upon the fact that believers are children of God and in his family (3:1–2; 5:1–2).

Other words besides *fellowship* (1:3, 6–7) that are prominent in the letter are *know*, which occurs about forty times, and *love*, which occurs fifty-two times in various forms as a noun, a verb, a participle, an adjective, and so forth. Four times John uses the expression *these things write we unto you*, with slight variation (1:4; 2:1; 2:26; 5:13).

Although the letter is difficult to outline, it seems to be built upon three expressions. Two of these describe God: "God is light" (1:5) and "God is love" (4:8, 16). Those who believe in the Lord Jesus Christ are "the children of God" (3:1, literal translation) and thus should participate in both his righteousness (light) and his love. Consequently, the outline might be:

1. INTRODUCTION: STATEMENT OF THE THEME—FELLOWSHIP IN THE FATHER'S FAMILY (1:1–4)

2. FELLOWSHIP WITH GOD WHO IS LIGHT (1:5–2:29)

3. THE CHILDREN OF GOD BY HIS LOVE (3:1–4:6)

4. FELLOWSHIP WITH GOD WHO IS LOVE (4:7–5:12)

5. CONCLUSION: PURPOSE OF WRITING AND CLOSING EXHORTATION (5:13–21)

2 JOHN

Again, as in 1 John, the writer does not identify himself by name. Here he calls himself "the elder" (verse 1; compare 1 Peter 5:1). There is ample evidence in this brief letter itself that it was written by the same man who wrote the gospel of John and the first letter. Note the references to truth (1–4; compare 1 John 1:6, 8; 2:21, 27; John 8:32; 14:6; 17:17; 18:37–38); to love (verse 5; compare 1 John 2:7; 4:7; John 13:34–35; 15:12,17); the reference to "Jesus Christ . . . in the flesh" (verse 7; compare 1 John 4:2–3; John 1:14; 20:31); and the use of the term *antichrist* (verse 7; compare 1 John 2:22; 4:3).

The address of the letter to "the elect lady and her children" (verse 1) has been thought by some to be a reference to a local church. It is more likely that this was a well-known Christian woman with whose family John was personally acquainted. By implication, of course, the letter is for all believers. It was probably written about the same time as

1 John. The occasion for writing this letter seems to have been the presence of false teachers (verse 7), against whom John warns. In this respect, this brief letter is similar to 2 Peter 2, 1 Timothy 4, and Jude.

Two prominent words in the letter are *truth* (verses 1–4) and *love* (verses 1, 3, 5–6).

"Truth" is viewed as the body of teaching that believers have received from God. It is also called "the doctrine of Christ" (verse 9). A prominent thought in the letter is that this truth is definite and limited, and that it includes all error. All teachers and teachings are to be tested by it. The letter may be outlined in this way:

1. KNOWING THE TRUTH (verses 1–3)

2. WALKING IN THE TRUTH (verses 4–6)

3. UPHOLDING THE TRUTH AGAINST DECEIVERS (verses 7–13)

Those who believe and maintain the truth of God must not compromise with error and must do nothing that would aid or comfort those who spread false teaching.

3 JOHN

This letter, also written by "the elder" (verse 1), is addressed to a Christian named Gaius (verse 1), but, of course, may be extended by implication to address any believer in Christ.

Apparently John had written to the church of which Gaius was a member (verse 9), but his letter had gone unheeded because of a man named Diotrephes, who was usurping authority and speaking evil of the apostle (verses 9–10). He writes this personal letter to Gaius to show that believers should have fellowship with all those who are maintaining a testimony for the truth. The letter may be outlined according to the three persons named in it:

1. GAIUS, WHO WALKED IN THE TRUTH (verses 1–8)

2. DIOTREPHES, WHO RESISTED THE TRUTH (verses 9–11)

3. DEMETRIUS, WHO HAD A GOOD REPORT OF THE TRUTH (verses 12–14)

The Gospel of Christ, which is exclusive in that it rules out all teachings contrary to it, is inclusive in the sense that it unites all of those who believe and promulgate it.

JUDE

The writer calls himself "Jude, the servant of Jesus Christ, and brother of James" (verse 1). This identifies him, along with James, as a half-brother of the Lord Jesus (compare Matthew 13:55; Mark 6:3; Galatians 1:19; John 7:3–5). The letter is addressed to Christians generally and probably was written around the year A.D. 70. Since it bears some similarity to 2 Peter and refers to the words "of the apostles of our Lord Jesus Christ" (verse 17), it must have been written after the letter, as well as after Paul's epistles.

The occasion of this letter was the apostasy, the falling away from the faith, which had already set in. There are several parallels between this letter and 2 Peter 2 concerning the description of false teachers.

The theme, as expressed in the letter itself, is "Contending for the Faith": "Beloved, while I was very diligent to write to you conerning our common salvation, I found it necessary to write to you exhorting you to contend earnestly for the faith which was once for all delivered to the saints" (verse 3

NKJV). While the full seriousness of the false teachers and their teachings is recognized, there is emphasis upon the power of God to keep those who belong to him (note especially verses 1, 24). The letter may be divided into four paragraphs:

1. INTRODUCTION AND EXHORTATION (verses 1–4)

This may be epitomized by the word *contend* (verse 3).

2. HISTORICAL EXAMPLES OF APOSTASY
    (verses 5–7)

This section may be remembered by the use of the word *remembrance* (verse 5).

3. DESCRIPTION OF FALSE TEACHERS (verses 8–19)

A designating word here is *woe* (verse 11).

4. INSTRUCTION AND COMFORT (verses 20–25)

Here the great word is *keep* (verses 21, 24).

8

The Final Prophecy— Revelation

In view of the title of the last book of the Bible, it is strange that many people consider it to be sealed. God calls it "The Revelation of Jesus Christ," his unveiling of things that must soon come to pass. This is the climactic book of prophecy, which explains and amplifies many of the things set forth in Daniel and other portions of the Old Testament. L. S. Chafer spoke of it as the great union station of prophecy, into which all the trunk lines from all parts of the Bible converge. The many symbols used are taken from the Old Testament. Although there is not one formal quotation from the Old Testament, the book is filled with references or allusions to it.

The human writer is John, the apostle, the writer of the fourth gospel and of the three letters of John. At the time God gave him this revelation, "the beloved disciple" was a prisoner on the island of Patmos, off the coast of Asia Minor, because of his faith in Christ. It is probable that this was the time of the persecution under the emperor Domitian, and the book was probably written about the year A.D. 95.

There have been four main schools of interpretation of Revelation. These are the *preterist,* which holds that the greater part of the book was fulfilled in the early history of the church; the *historical,* which views the entire book as being fulfilled during the present age; *futurist,* which considers that the greater part of the book pertains to events in the end time, shortly before the return of the Lord; and the *idealist,* which sees the book merely as symbolic of the conflict between good and evil, without reference to specific time.

The view set forth in this book is futurist.

The Lord himself outlines the book in his words to John: "Write the things which you have seen, and the things which are, and the things which shall be hereafter" (1:19). Hence, the three main divisions of the book are as follows:

1. THE VISION OF THE GLORIFIED CHRIST—"THE THINGS WHICH YOU HAVE SEEN" (chapter 1)

2. THE LETTERS TO THE SEVEN CHURCHES— "THE THINGS WHICH ARE" (chapters 2–3)

3. END-TIMES EVENTS—"THE THINGS WHICH SHALL BE HEREAFTER" (chapters 4–22)

A special blessing is pronounced upon the one who reads and observes this book (1:3). Part of this blessing, no doubt, is the fact that, in order to understand Revelation, one must have a knowledge of all parts of the Word of God. Of course, the primary meaning of the verse is that the one who hears and obeys the book will not be overtaken by the judgment that God is to bring upon the earth.

1. The Vision of the Glorified Christ (chapter 1)

The Lord Jesus Christ appears in glory to the apostle John as the one who is to judge all men. The marvelous symbolic description of him points out the fact of judgment. He is seen in the midst of the churches, first judging those who claim to be his own people (chapters 2–3) and then judging the world (chapters 4–20).

2. The Letters to the Seven Churches (chapters 2–3)

These letters are addressed to seven literal, local churches in the Roman province of Asia, a portion of what we today call Asia Minor. This is their primary meaning. They have, of course, a general application in that all of them together make up the different kinds of conditions found in the church at large. Evidently there is also a prophetic meaning to the letters in that, together, they give a resume of church history during the present age. Hence, in the prophetic sense, Ephesus represents the church at the close of the apostolic age in John's own day. Smyrna is the church of the persecution. Pergamos, or Pergamum, is the church in the period when it became recognized by the Roman Empire. Thyatira represents the papal church; Sardis, nominal and dead Protestantism following the period of the Reformation. Philadelphia is the true church within the professing church (note the promise in 3:10); and Laodicea, the lukewarm church of the end time. It is no doubt significant that the first three of these are grouped together in that the admonition to "hear" precedes the promise to the overcomer. In the last four this order is reversed and each of the four letters includes a mention of the return of the Lord, no doubt indicating that while they began at different times, all four of these conditions continue until the end of the age.

3. End-Time Events (chapters 4–22)

One who reads the book of Revelation cannot help noticing that it includes a number of series of sevens. The four most prominent are the seven churches, the seven seals, the seven trumpets, and the seven vials (or bowls). The first of these, the seven churches, is found, of course, in chapters 2 and 3. The other three series of sevens are found in the third main division of the book. There is difference of opinion among Bible interpreters concerning the relationship of the seals, the trumpets, and the bowls. Some believe that they are successive (figure 1); others believe that they are contemporaneous (figure 2). A more likely view is that they are overlapping, meaning that the seventh seal includes all that follows in the seven trumpets, and that the seventh trumpet includes all that follows in the seven bowls (figure 3).

The description of the seven seals extends from 4:1–8:1. John is first introduced to the heavenly scene (chapters 4–5). Here he sees the throne of God, symbolic of God's government and his judgment of the earth. The heavenly beings praise God because of creation (chapter 4). Next John sees the seven-sealed book and discovers that the Lamb, who is also the Lion of the tribe of Judah, is the only one worthy to open it. This book represents the coming judgments of God upon the earth. The Lord Jesus Christ is the judge (compare John 5:22, 27; Acts 17:31).

In each of the three series—the seals, the trumpets, and the bowls—there is an interlude or parenthesis between the sixth and the seventh of the series. It is likely that the judgments of the first six seals take place during the first half of Daniel's seventieth week. (For the "seventy weeks," or seventy sevens of years, see Daniel 9:24–27). In the inter-

Figure 1—Successive

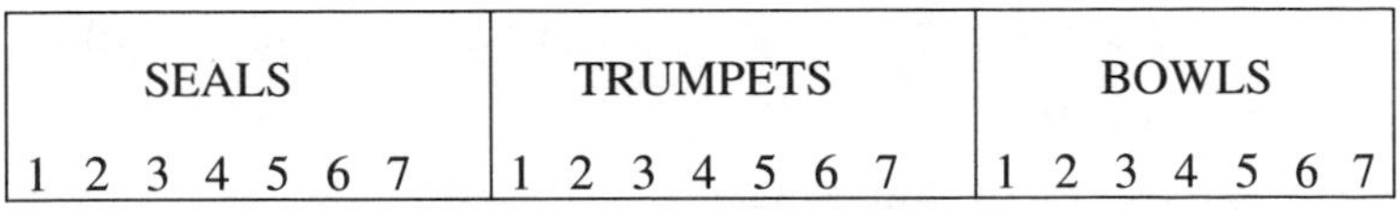

SEALS	TRUMPETS	BOWLS
1 2 3 4 5 6 7	1 2 3 4 5 6 7	1 2 3 4 5 6 7

Figure 2—Contemporaneous

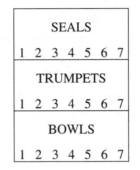

SEALS

1 2 3 4 5 6 7

TRUMPETS

1 2 3 4 5 6 7

BOWLS

1 2 3 4 5 6 7

Figure 3—Overlapping

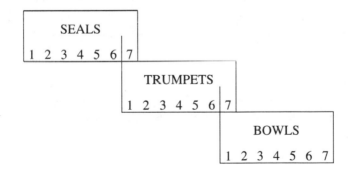

SEALS

1 2 3 4 5 6 | 7

TRUMPETS

1 2 3 4 5 6 | 7

BOWLS

1 2 3 4 5 6 7

lude between the sixth and the seventh seals, John is permitted to see the great company of those who will be saved during "the great tribulation" (7:14 ASV): the 144,000 will be the godly remnant of Israel during the tribulation period (7:4–8); a great multitude of Gentiles will be saved in that awful time (7:9–17).

The breaking of the seventh seal introduces the seven trumpets. In these, the judgments become more intensified. It has been suggested by many interpreters that the judgments under the seals are indirect in that many of the calamities come about through human agencies, and that the judgments under the trumpets are also indirect, being caused to a large extent by satanic and demonic agencies. Note especially the locusts under the fifth trumpet (9:1–12). It is probable that these represent the great host of demons controlled by Satan. Another interlude comes between the sixth and the seventh trumpets (10:1–11:14). The events of chapters 12 and 13 seem to cover the same period described in the trumpets. Many believe that the casting of Satan out of heaven, which comes at the middle of Daniel's seventieth week (12:9), is parallel in time to the blowing of the fifth trumpet (9:1). The latter half of the seventieth week is the time known specifically as "the great tribulation." This tribulation is described in these chapters. Satan, the dragon, persecutes the woman, Israel, because he cannot get at the Manchild, the Lord Jesus Christ. The two beasts (chapter 13) join with Satan to form a grotesque and terrible counterfeit of the Holy Trinity—the dragon, the beast, and the false prophet. The first beast is the world ruler of the end time, the one described in Daniel 7 as the little horn. He is the Antichrist who takes from Satan's hand that which the Lord Jesus Christ had repudiated, the control of the world through the worship of the devil. Before the final judgments of God in the vials or bowls are poured out, John sees again the

Lamb, the Lord Jesus Christ, with his elect company from Israel (14:1–5), and hears the announcement of the fall of Babylon (14:8), the great God-defying world system described more fully in later chapters.

The judgments of the vials, or literally bowls, are direct visitations of God's wrath upon the earth (15:1) and are more severe than the judgments which preceded. At the pouring out of the seventh bowl Babylon falls. In chapters 17 and 18 we are given a more detailed description of this fall. Here we see the woman called *Babylon,* the terrible counterfeit of the true bride of Christ, as the apostate religious system of the end time, at first controlling the kingdoms of this world and later destroyed by them. There is little doubt that the description specifically fits the city of Rome (17:9) and that both the false religious system and the false governmental system described in chapter 18 have their headquarters there. The fall of political Babylon (chapter 18) is reminiscent of the destruction of the image of Gentile world power in Daniel 2.

The second coming of Christ in glory is described in chapter 19. This is to be distinguished from the rapture of the church, which is not specifically mentioned in Revelation since this book, from chapter 4 on, deals with God's judgments upon Israel and the Gentile nations. Other passages of Scripture show that the rapture of the Church is imminent, that the Lord Jesus may appear at any moment to receive his own unto himself before these terrible events of the end time break upon the world.

When the Lord Jesus comes in glory, Antichrist and his followers will actually be arrogant and audacious enough to think that they can repel the Lord. This so-called battle of Armageddon is not a battle at all in the ordinary sense, for the Lord Jesus Christ will destroy his enemies with the brightness of his coming (2 Thessalonians 2:8).

The twentieth chapter of Revelation is one of the most crucial passages in Scripture because of its mention of the thousand-year reign of Christ and his followers upon the earth. Among believers who hold to a literal return of the Lord Jesus Christ to the earth, there have been three different schools of thought. The *premillennialists* hold that the Lord Jesus Christ will come personally to set up his Kingdom and to reign for a period of one-thousand years upon the earth. This is the literal interpretation of the passage. More than fifty extended passages of the Old Testament speak of a future kingdom for Israel upon the earth. The *postmillennialist* view holds that, through the preaching of the gospel, a time of peace and prosperity will come upon the earth, after which the Lord Jesus Christ will come for the final judgment. The *amillennial* view is the belief that there will be no literal earthly Kingdom, but that the thousand-year period refers to the present age, that all of the prophecies of a future kingdom on the earth are fulfilled spiritually in the church. This amillennial view requires that the first resurrection be interpreted spiritually, but in Revelation 20 two resurrections are mentioned (compare John 5:29). It would seem strange that one should be literal and the other not. Besides, resurrection in the Scripture is always of the body. This period of the Millennium, the thousand-year reign of Christ, will be followed by the loosing of Satan and the final revolt that shows the depravity of sinful humanity, even after the personal reign of Christ. Scripture teaches that hell, the lake of fire, is a terrible reality.

The last two chapters describe the new heaven and the new earth and the glories of the eternal state. Our understanding is too limited to comprehend all that God has for us, but we rejoice in the hope of his glory.

The Lord Jesus Christ, who has given this great message to John through his angel, speaks again personally at the close (22:16), giving a tender and loving invitation: "And let him that is thirsty come. And whosoever will, let him take the water of life freely" (22:17).

We are reminded again at the close of the book, as at the beginning, of the imminent coming of the Lord Jesus Christ. May our hearts respond as John's did, "Even so, come, Lord Jesus" (22:20).

Maps of Paul's Journeys

PAUL'S FIRST MISSIONARY JOURNEY

PAUL'S SECOND MISSIONARY JOURNEY

PAUL'S THIRD MISSIONARY JOURNEY

PAUL'S JOURNEY TO ROME

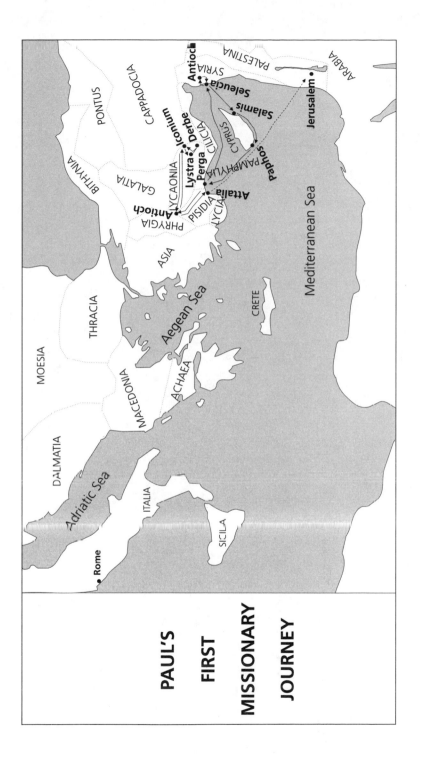

PAUL'S FIRST MISSIONARY JOURNEY

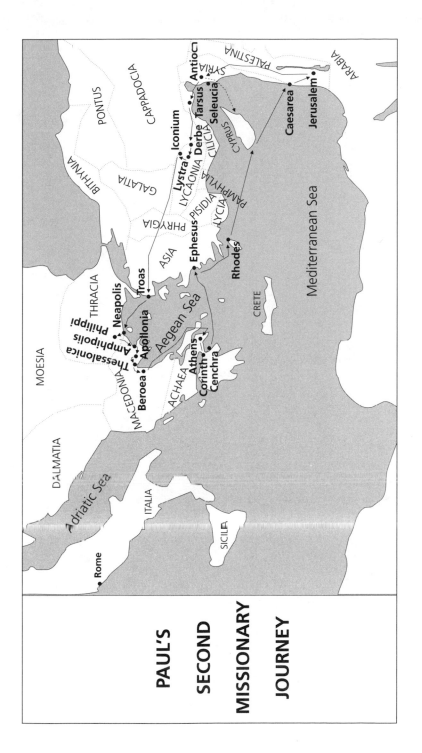

PAUL'S
SECOND
MISSIONARY
JOURNEY

PONTUS

CAPPADOCIA

BITHYNIA

GALATIA

Iconium
Lystra
Derbe
LYCAONIA

Antioch
Tarsus
Seleucia
SYRIA
CILICIA
PALESTINA

Caesarea

Jerusalem

ARABIA

CYPRUS

PAMPHYLIA
PISIDIA
PHRYGIA
LYCIA
ASIA

Ephesus

Rhodes

Troas
Neapolis
THRACIA
Apollonia
Philippi
Amphipolis
Thessalonica
MACEDONIA
Beroea
Athens
Corinth
Cenchra
ACHAEA

Aegean Sea

CRETE

Mediterranean Sea

MOESIA

DALMATIA

Adriatic Sea

ITALIA

Rome

SICILIA

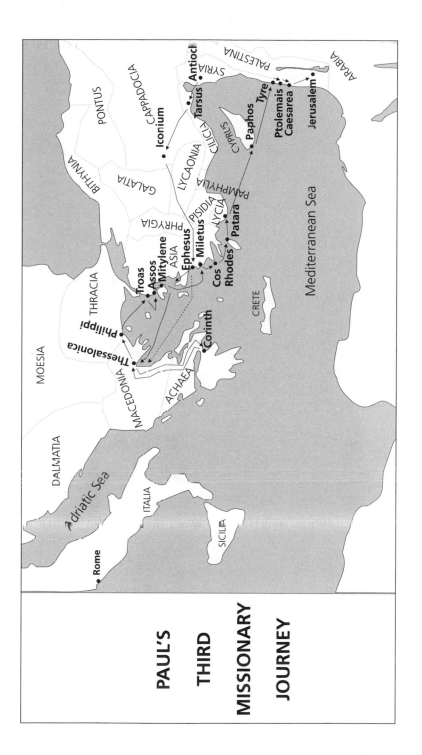

PAUL'S

THIRD

MISSIONARY

JOURNEY

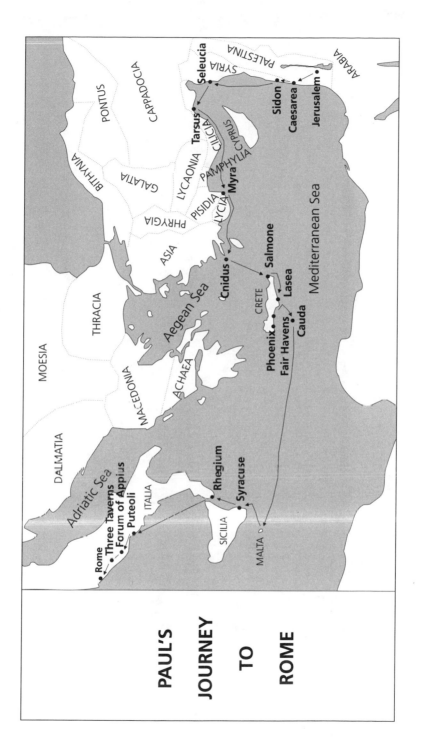

PAUL'S
JOURNEY
TO
ROME

The New
Testament

Matthew through Revelation